Cabaret

Series Editor: Barry Monush

Cabaret

Stephen Tropiano

AN IMPRINT OF HAL LEONARD CORPORATION

Published in 2011 by Limelight Editions
An Imprint of Hal Leonard Corporation
7777 West Bluemound Road
Milwaukee, WI 53213

Trade Book Division Editorial Offices
33 Plymouth Street, Suite 302, Montclair, NJ 07042

Printed in the United States of America

Book design by Mark Lerner

Library of Congress Cataloging-in-Publication Data is available upon request.

ISBN 978-0-87910-382-8

www.limelighteditions.com

CONTENTS

ACKNOWLEDGMENTS

For taking the time to share their recollections and answer my questions, thanks to Joel Grey, Vic Heutschy, John Kander, Liza Minnelli, and Louise Quick.

For their invaluable assistance with this project, thanks to David Arthur, Rebecca Bilek-Chee, Sylvia Borchert, John Calhoun, Brian Codling, Michael Dolan, Scott Ellis, Scott Gorenstein, Maarten Kooij, Kevin LaVine, Michael Messina, Linda Mizejewski, Rosemary Rotondi, and Deborah Silberberg.

For their friendship and support, thanks to Jon Bassinger-Flores, Matthew Jon Beck, Linda Bobel, Faith Ginsberg, Gary Jones, Ray Morton, Luke Reichle, Barry Sandler, Neil Spisak, Arnold Stiefel, and Holly Van Buren.

A major thank you to my agent, June Clark; John Cerullo; Barry Monush; and Bernadette Malavarca and Marybeth Keating at Limelight Editions.

As always, thanks to Steven G.

The book was made possible in part by a James B. Pendleton Grant from the Roy H. Park School of Communications at Ithaca College.

A portion of the author's proceeds will be donated to The Trevor Project, a nonprofit organization that operates the Trevor Lifeline, a national twenty-four-hour crisis and suicide prevention helpline for lesbian, gay, bisexual, transgender, and questioning youth (866-4-U-TREVOR). Visit their Web site at www.thetrevorproject.org.

Cabaret

CHAPTER 1

"Willkommen, Bienvenue, Welcome"

On February 15, 1972, the *Hollywood Reporter* published one of the first of many rave reviews of the eagerly awaited movie musical, *Cabaret*. According to critic Gary Giddins, "*Cabaret* is a stunning entertainment, an exuberant marriage of talent and intelligence. Conceptually, it is a musical that will even please people who don't particularly care for musicals."

A musical for people who don't particularly care for musicals?

There is no doubt that a large segment of the movie-going public can't help but shudder or scoff at the sight of a grown man bursting into song or tap dancing in the rain. With the exception of the horror film, no other genre polarizes Hollywood audiences more than the musical.

Musicals are like horror movies: you either love them or hate them.

On the surface, *Cabaret* is typical of most movie musicals of the period. The film is based on a popular stage musical that ran on Broadway for over two and a half years (November 20, 1966–September 6, 1969) and 1,165 performances. In the 1960s, Hollywood produced an unprecedented number of stage-to-screen adaptations, several of which scored with the critics, audiences, and Oscar voters. Between 1960 and 1969, four of the 10 Academy Award winners for Best Picture were screen adaptations of successful stage musicals: *West Side Story* (1961), *My Fair Lady* (1964), *The Sound of Music* (1965), and *Oliver!* (1968). Together they received a combined total of 44 nominations and 29 Oscars. *The Sound of Music* even surpassed *Gone with the Wind* (1939) as the all-time box-office champ, earning approximately $135 million.

At the time, Hollywood studios were willing to pay top dollar for the screen rights to a long-running Broadway musical because its commercial potential had already been tested and its instant title recognition made the film easier to market. In hopes of repeating the box-office success of *The Sound of Music*, the studios sank millions of dollars into a string of both big-budget stage-to-screen adaptations and original musicals that tanked at the box office: *Doctor Dolittle* (1967), *Camelot* (1967), *Star!* (1968), *Chitty Chitty*

Bang Bang (1968), *Goodbye, Mr. Chips* (1969), *Sweet Charity* (1969), *Paint Your Wagon* (1969), and *Darling Lili* (1970). With production costs on the rise, a musical was considered a risky business venture when Allied Artists secured the film rights to the stage musical *Cabaret* for $1.5 million. To cover the cost of production, Allied made a deal with ABC Pictures to split the film's projected $5 million budget.

A film version of *Cabaret* also posed a potential financial risk because Hollywood musicals generally catered to a family audience. The story is set in Berlin, in 1931, during the rise of fascism, which is a far cry from the carefree, Technicolor utopian settings of MGM musicals like *An American in Paris* (1951), *Singin' in the Rain* (1952), and *The Band Wagon* (1953), or more recent big-budget spectacles like *Doctor Dolittle* and *Hello, Dolly!* (1969). In addition, *Cabaret* deals with adult subject matter and themes, such as National Socialism, anti-Semitism, and abortion—not exactly standard fare for a Hollywood musical.

At the helm of *Cabaret*'s transition from the stage to the screen was director/choreographer Bob Fosse, whose credits included such Broadway hits as *The Pajama Game* (1954), *Damn Yankees* (1955), and *How to Succeed in Business Without Really Trying* (1961). Unfortunately, his first film, an over-budget, overdone, high-gloss screen version of *Sweet Charity*, a musical he originally directed and choreographed for the Broadway stage, was a critical and box-office failure. But Fosse had no intention of turning *Cabaret* into another *Sweet Charity*. What he envisioned instead was a musical in the style of a European art film, which, since the late 1960s, had influenced a new wave of American moviemaking known as the New Hollywood Cinema. A young generation of filmmakers that included Arthur Penn (*Bonnie and Clyde* [1967]), Martin Scorsese (*Taxi Driver* [1976]), Mike Nichols (*The Graduate* [1967]), John Schlesinger (*Midnight Cowboy* [1969]), Robert Altman (*Nashville* [1975]), Hal Ashby (*Harold and Maude* [1971]), and Peter Bogdanovich (*The Last Picture Show* [1971]) worked within the studio system, yet their films were not made in the classical Hollywood style. Shooting on location instead of a studio back lot, they intentionally broke the rules by experimenting, in a highly self-conscious manner, with narrative, editing, and sound. Thematically, in the spirit of the 1960s counterculture, many of these films also went against the grain by challenging dominant American values, beliefs, and traditions.

For some people, the main criterion for a successful screen adaptation of a Broadway musical is how faithful the film remains to the original. But Fosse and his collaborators were not interested in merely reproducing what had been done onstage, so they made some bold and risky choices in adapting *Cabaret*. Two thirds of John Kander and Fred Ebb's Tony Award-winning score was tossed out, along with two main characters and one major plotline. The most radical change involved the musical numbers, all of which, with one important exception, would be limited to performances on the stage of the Kit Kat Klub by singer Sally Bowles, the Emcee, and the Kit Kat Girls. This change, combined with Fosse's art house aesthetics and the film's treatment of mature themes, broadened the musical's appeal among adults.

While *Cabaret* jump-started Fosse's directing career, the film was a genuine star turn for its leading lady, Liza Minnelli. Her previous work on stage and in films did not go unnoticed. She won her first Tony at the age of nineteen for her Broadway debut in *Flora, the Red Menace* (1965), and received Oscar, British Academy, and Golden Globe nominations for her role as a quirky college student in *The Sterile Cuckoo* (1969). But it was her portrayal of Sally Bowles that set off a media frenzy and catapulted her to international stardom. *Cabaret* premiered in New York on February 13, 1972. Two weeks later, Liza appeared on the covers of both *Time* ("The New Miss Show Biz—Liza Minnelli") and *Newsweek* ("Liza Minnelli in 'Cabaret'—A Star is Born"). Both articles, and the dozens of others that followed, discussed her show business background, particularly her relationship with her late mother, Judy Garland, and father, film director Vincente Minnelli, yet emphasized that she was an original talent, and not a carbon copy of her mother.

Cabaret redefined the Hollywood musical by infusing the genre with an art house sensibility and experimenting with its conventions, particularly the integration of the musical's three key elements—story, song, and dance. Fosse's innovative direction, the stellar performances of Minnelli and her costars Joel Grey, Michael York, and Marisa Berenson, and, of course, a terrific score by John Kander and Fred Ebb proved to be a winning combination both artistically and financially for the filmmakers. The musical grossed over $40 million at the box office and cleaned up during the 1972–73 award season, receiving 10 Academy Award nominations and winning eight, including Best Director (Fosse), Best Actress (Minnelli), and Best Supporting Actor (Grey).

This book chronicles the story behind the film *Cabaret*, from the novel that introduced Miss Sally Bowles to the world, Christopher Isherwood's *Goodbye to Berlin*, to its various incarnations that preceded the 1972 film, including the stage and screen versions of *I Am a Camera*, by John Van Druten, and the 1966 Broadway musical on which *Cabaret* is based. In the process, it celebrates the people and their artistry that made *Cabaret* not only a memorable musical but also a musical for people who don't particularly care for musicals.

CHAPTER 2

Chris and Sally
On the Page, Stage, and Screen

The story behind the story of *Cabaret* begins, like the film, with the arrival of a young British writer to Weimar Berlin.

The writer, Christopher William Bradshaw Isherwood, was born in 1904 in Cheshire, England into an upper middle-class family. His father, Frank, a lieutenant colonel in the British Army, was killed in 1915 at the second Battle of Ypres, leaving Isherwood and his younger brother, Richard, to be raised by their mother, Kathleen. Isherwood attended preparatory school, where he met a lifelong friend and occasional collaborator, British poet W. H. Auden, who, several years later, would introduce Isherwood to Berlin's "gay" (as in "homosexual") scene. Isherwood received a scholarship to Cambridge University, but by his second year he grew bored with his studies and was expelled for deliberately failing his exams, which afforded him more time to devote to his writing.

In the fall of 1929, when twenty-five-year-old Isherwood stepped off the train at Berlin Friedrichstraße, he had published his first novel, *All the Conspirators* (1928), and translated the *Intimate Journals* of French writer Charles Baudelaire. His own intimate journals, in which he recorded his experiences in Berlin between the years 1929 and 1933, would later be the basis for two short novels, *Mr. Norris Changes Trains* (1935) (published simultaneously in the United States under the title *The Last of Mr. Norris*), and *Goodbye to Berlin* (1939). In 1945, New Directions, the American publisher of the early works of such controversial writers as Jorge Luis Borges, Vladimir Nabokov, and Henry Miller, released both novels as a single volume under the title *The Berlin Stories*.

Goodbye to Berlin is not a traditional novel. It comprises six self-contained, loosely connected stories set in the final years of the Weimar Republic (1918–33). The novel's first-person narrator is a British writer named Christopher Isherwood, leading many readers to mistake *Goodbye* for an autobiography. As Isherwood once explained, *Goodbye to Berlin* is based on his experiences living in Berlin, yet he fictionalized them to make the stories "more coherent and indeed *truer*." (To avoid confusion, I will refer to the fictional narrator of *Goodbye to Berlin* as "Christopher" and the novel's real author as "Isherwood.")

The other characters in *Goodbye to Berlin* are all based on real people. According to Isherwood, to turn a real person into a fictional character, a writer should emphasize the individual's most interesting qualities, play loose with the facts, and invent situations that did not necessarily occur. That's exactly what Isherwood did when he created the colorful characters who would later be brought to life in the stage/film versions of *I Am a Camera* (1951/1955) and *Cabaret* (1966/1972), including one of the most original female characters to grace the printed page, the Broadway stage, and the big screen: a free-spirited cabaret singer named Sally Bowles.

Isherwood's Berlin

Although it is a work of fiction, *Goodbye to Berlin* is an insightful portrait of Berlin life during a tumultuous period in Germany's history that marked the end of the Weimar Republic and paved the way for the rise of the National Socialists to power. When Isherwood arrived in the city in 1929, Germany was a country in crisis. The "Golden Years" of the Weimar Republic (1925–29) ended when the Wall Street crash of 1929 destabilized the German economy by shutting off the supply of short-term loans from American investors to Germany. Consequently, factories closed their doors and the unemployment rate soared. At the same time, the Nazis were steadily gaining power by exploiting the German people's hatred and distrust of the collapsing Weimar government and by blaming the current economic crisis on Jewish bankers. The poverty, unemployment, and political tensions remain mostly in the background of *Goodbye to Berlin* until the final episode, "A Berlin Diary (Winter 1932–3)," in which Christopher leaves Berlin soon after Hitler is sworn in as chancellor (on January 30, 1933), marking the official start of the Nazis' reign of terror.

"The sun shines," wrote Isherwood, "and Hitler is master of this city."

The Nazi Party's rise to power also marked the end of the great cultural revolution that had transformed post–World War I Germany into the international epicenter for artistic innovation, scientific discovery, and intellectual thought. Berlin in particular was a cultural playground for painters, poets, musicians, composers, writers, entertainers, and filmmakers. The influence of modernism was evident in the liberating sound of jazz, the architectural designs of the Bauhaus School, and the haunting imagery of Otto Dix, George Grosz, and other members of the New Objectivity art movement.

In the 1920s, Berlin was home to such notable artists as film director Fritz Lang (*Metropolis* [1927], *M* [1931]), dramatist Bertolt Brecht and composer Kurt Weill (*Die*

Dreigroschenoper [*The Threepenny Opera*] [1928]), novelist Erich Maria Remarque (*Im Westen nichts Neues* [*All Quiet on the Western Front*] [1929]), and a host of intellectuals, philosophers, and scientists, including physicist Albert Einstein and sexologist/gay rights pioneer Dr. Magnus Hirschfeld. All of these men and many others (most of whom were Jewish) were forced to flee Germany in the 1930s when the Nazis declared war on what they called *entartete Kunst* (degenerate art) on the grounds it was un-German and part of the so-called Jewish–Bolshevik conspiracy against the Aryan race. "Subversive" books were publicly burned, "degenerate" artistic expression in any form was banned, and Jewish professors and students were barred from universities.

Another aspect of Berlin culture that fell victim to the Nazis was the Berlin cabaret, a popular form of stage entertainment consisting of musical acts and comical sketches. Historian Peter Jelavich contends that the images most Americans have of the Berlin cabarets of the 1920s are based on the songs of Bertolt Brecht and Kurt Weill and the films *The Blue Angel* (1930), starring Marlene Dietrich as singer Lola Lola, and *Cabaret*. Jelavich explains that Brecht, Weill, Lola Lola, and Sally Bowles "were, in short, on the boundaries of cabaret. And those boundaries were fluid." He describes the "ideal cabaret" of the period as an intimate setting with a small stage, where a series of satirical or parodistic songs, comic monologues, and skits that dealt with topical issues (sex, politics, cultural fads, etc.) were performed. As seen in *Cabaret*, there was an emcee who introduced each act and interacted with the audience.

　Surprisingly, the cabaret world is not prominently featured in Isherwood's stories. The character of Sally Bowles in *Goodbye to Berlin* is an aspiring singer/actress whom Christopher watches perform in what he describes as "an arty 'informal' bar" called The Lady Windermere (so named after Oscar Wilde's 1892 play, *Lady Windermere's Fan*). Christopher is not impressed with the establishment, and at the end of the evening he vows "never to visit a place of this sort again."

He doesn't keep his promise. Prior to his departure from Berlin, he accompanies his friend Fritz on a "tour of 'the dives,'" which includes The Salomé, a gay and lesbian cabaret that caters to the tourist trade. Christopher describes it as a "very expensive and even more depressing than I had imagined," and after watching "a young man in a spangled crinoline and jeweled breast-caps" perform three splits on stage, he and Fritz head for the door. Outside they are approached by a group of drunken American youths, one of whom asks Fritz if this is a queer bar.

"Eventually we're all queer," responds Fritz, a heterosexual.

Another youth asks Christopher if he is queer. "Yes," Christopher replies, "very queer indeed."

Although both Fritz and Christopher seem to be getting some perverse pleasure out of playing with the drunken youths, Christopher's remark was perhaps Isherwood's way of alluding to what *Goodbye to Berlin* never directly addresses: the sexuality of his literary alter ego, who, despite the sexual permissiveness that pervaded Weimar Berlin and made it a popular tourist attraction for people of all sexual persuasions, remains asexual throughout the novel.

Berlin's rich cultural climate no doubt attracted Isherwood to the city, yet there is another reason he called it home for three years. "Berlin meant boys," Isherwood candidly admitted thirty-five years later in his 1976 memoir, *Christopher and His Kind*, in which he revealed that he returned to Berlin after a short visit because of the sexually available young men he discovered behind the "heavy leather curtain door" of a gay bar called the Cozy Corner. Isherwood claimed that like many upper-class homosexuals, he was unable to "relax sexually with a member of his own class or nation" and felt more comfortable with a "working-class foreigner." There is no mention of Isherwood's lovers or sexual liaisons in *Goodbye to Berlin*, though he later revealed that Otto Nowak, the bisexual German teenager who is featured prominently in two of the Berlin short stories, was his lover. Although homosexuality was illegal at the time under Paragraph 175 of the German Criminal Code, the law was not enforced in the liberal political climate of Weimar Germany. Consequently, Berlin offered tourists, the curious, and pleasure seekers like Isherwood a wide choice of gay, lesbian, and transvestite establishments. This would all soon change once the Nazis came into power and broadened the law with harsher penalties, resulting in an increase in arrests and prosecutions, the closing of Berlin's gay bars, and the eventual imprisonment of homosexuals.

The Real Sally Bowles: Jean Ross

In December 1930, Isherwood moved to the Schöneberg district of Berlin near Nollendorfplatz, one of the oldest gay neighborhoods in the city. He rented a room in a flat at Nollendorfstrasse 17, outside of which there now hangs a plaque written in German (translated in English below) commemorating Isherwood and the residence's connection to his fiction and the musical *Cabaret*:

HERE, BETWEEN MARCH 1929 AND JAN/FEB 1933

LIVED THE ENGLISH WRITER

CHRISTOPHER ISHERWOOD

* 26. 8. 1904   † 5. 1. 1986

HIS NOVELS "GOODBYE TO BERLIN" AND

"MR. NORRIS CHANGES TRAINS"

ARE BASED ON HIS EXPERIENCE DURING THIS PERIOD.

INSPIRED BY BOTH OF THESE NOVELS,
THE MUSICAL "CABARET" WAS CREATED.

The people Isherwood met during his three-year stay in Berlin were indeed the inspiration for the characters he would later bring to life, including *Cabaret*'s leading lady.

In the chapter of *Goodbye to Berlin* entitled "Sally Bowles," Christopher describes the nineteen-year-old British cabaret singer to whom he is introduced by his friend Fritz Wendel:

> She was dressed in black silk, with a small cape over her shoulders and a little cap like a page-boy's stuck jauntily on one side of her head. . . . I noticed that her finger-nails were painted emerald green, a colour unfortunately chosen, for it called attention to her hands, which were much stained by cigarette-smoking and as dirty as a little girl's.

The next time Christopher saw Sally she was singing at the Lady Windermere "in a surprisingly deep husky voice." "She sang badly, without any expression," Christopher observed, "her hands hanging down at her sides—yet her performance was, in its own way, effective because of her startling appearance and her air of not caring a curse what people thought of her." Thirty-five years later, Sally's lack of talent would be a point of contention when it came to casting the role in the stage and film versions of *Cabaret*.

In the novel, Christopher and Sally become fast friends, and once they reach a mutual understanding that neither is in love with the other, she moves into the same flat, into the room next to his. Soon afterward, Sally becomes involved with a man named Klaus, who takes a job in England and later sends a letter informing her that he is now engaged to an English aristocrat. Chris consoles the heartbroken Sally, who soon forgets her troubles when the pair begin to pal around with a rich American named Clive, who buys them expensive dinners and gifts. Clive promises to take them on a trip around the world, but changes his mind at the last minute and leaves town. The money included in Clive's goodbye note comes in handy when Sally discovers she's pregnant with Klaus' baby and must pay for an abortion. Once Sally recovers, Chris leaves Berlin for a few months. When he returns, his relationship with Sally, who has since moved out of the building, is strained and becomes even more so when she implies he lacks real talent as a writer. Sally's run-in with a con man reunites the pair, and with their friendship intact, Sally leaves Chris to pursue her acting career in Paris.

When one thinks of Fraulein Sally Bowles, the image that immediately comes to mind is Liza Minnelli in a black bowler hat, thigh-high boots, a black vest sans shirt, and bright red lipstick, standing with one foot on a chair. Although Julie Harris was the first to play the character in both the stage and film versions of *I Am a Camera*, it is Liza who will forever be associated with the role.

The character created by Isherwood and brought to life by Harris and Minnelli was modeled on a real person, a friend of Isherwood's named Jean Ross. According to Isherwood's biographer, Peter Parker, Ross was born in 1911 in Alexandria, Egypt to wealthy British parents. She had a rebellious streak and managed to get expelled from boarding school for lying to the headmistress, saying that she was pregnant. She attended the Royal Academy of Dramatic Arts for one year and was cast in a small part in a low-budget British film comedy, *Why Sailors Leave Home* (1930), before heading to Berlin, where she supported herself by singing and modeling. Ross also continued to act, playing the role of Anitra in a stage production of *Peer Gynt* directed by Max Reinhardt, an opportunity Minnelli's Sally would have died for.

Like her literary counterpart, Ross moved into a room in the same flat at Nollendorfstrasse 17 in 1931, though to Isherwood's recollection she remained there for only a few months. Unlike Sally's relationship with Cliff Bradshaw in the musical *Cabaret* and with Brian Roberts in the film, Ross and Isherwood's relationship was not sexual, yet, according to the writer, it was also "more truly intimate than the relationships between Sally and her various partners in the novel, the plays, and the films." Isherwood characterized his relationship with Ross as "the simplest imaginable. She knew that I was fond of her like a sister and that I was a contented homosexual. We had no problems."

There were some similarities between Ross and her literary counterpart: both were performers with limited musical talent, were sexually liberated women with a penchant for talking about their numerous lovers (though Isherwood believed Ross exaggerated the number of men), and had an illegal abortion. Years later, Isherwood admitted he came close to removing the "Sally Bowles" chapter from *Goodbye to Berlin* because Ross was concerned about her connection to the character in his novel and the fact she'd had an abortion. Before publishing *Goodbye to Berlin*, Isherwood sent copies of the manuscript to everyone who appears as a character and asked for their approval. Ross took two months before giving her consent, which put the matter to rest.

Although Isherwood was frequently asked over the years, he never revealed Sally's identity to the press, though it was known in certain circles that Ross was the model for Bowles, who was named after a mutual acquaintance living in Berlin at the time, American writer/composer Paul Bowles. Finally, in 1968, around the time the musical *Cabaret* opened in London, the British tabloid newspaper, the *Daily Mail*, tracked down Ross in London. In addition to working as an actress in the theater, Ross worked as a scenario writer in the German film industry, and like her husband, Claud Cockburn, she was an outspoken left-wing journalist with communist sympathies—a far cry from the apolitical Sally Bowles. Minnelli thinks this is "absolutely stunning" because "it's typical of the Sally Bowles character to do a complete reversal and get involved in politics!"

According to Ross' daughter, detective-story writer Sarah Caudwell, her mother never identified with the character, who she believed more closely resembled one of Isherwood's male friends. When a revival of the stage musical opened in London in 1986, Caudwell penned a piece for the British left-wing magazine *New Statesman* in which she claimed, "It was in Isherwood's life, not hers [her mother's] that Sally Bowles remained a significant figure." Ross was apparently also frustrated with journalists when they questioned her about Berlin in the 1930s. Caudwell explained that her mother would say, "They didn't want to know about the unemployment or the poverty or the Nazis marching through the streets—all they want to know is how many men I went to bed with. Really, darling, how on earth can anyone be interested in that?"

While Ross, at least according to her daughter, may have objected to Isherwood's characterization of her, the former housemates did maintain a friendship until her death in 1973. In *Christopher and His Kind*, Isherwood, writing in both the first person and third person (as the character "Christopher"), reflects on how his memories of Ross and his creation, Sally Bowles, are overshadowed by the actresses who brought the character to life on the stage and screen:

> I wish I could remember what impression Jean Ross . . . made on Christopher when they first met. But I can't. Art has transfigured life and other people's art has transfigured Christopher's art. . . . And both Sally and Jean keep being jostled to one side of my memory to make way for the actresses who have played the part of Sally on the stage and on the screen. These, regardless of their merits, are all much more vivid to me than either Jean or Sally; their boldly made-up, brightly lit faces are larger than life.

Isherwood's Cast of Characters

In addition to Christopher Isherwood and Sally Bowles, three additional characters—Fraulein Schneider, Fritz Wendel, and Natalia Landauer—were included when *Goodbye to Berlin* was adapted for the stage and screen versions of *I Am a Camera* and *Cabaret* (see table on pages 26 and 27).

Fraulein Schroeder, who is renamed Fraulein Schneider in *I Am a Camera* and *Cabaret*, is modeled after Isherwood's beloved landlady at Nollendorfstrasse 17, Fraulein Meta Thurau. Isherwood claimed that of all the characters, she is the "least distorted from the original," though Thurau did object to how he characterized her walk as a "waddle." Like Frl. Schroeder, Frl. Thurau was deeply fond of Isherwood, whom she addresses in *The Berlin Stories* as "Herr Issyvoo." When Christopher departs Berlin in the final story ("A Berlin Diary [Winter 1932-3]"), he describes Frl. Schroeder as "inconsolable." He also observes how, like many Germans, she was "acclimating" herself to the political changes. Although Isherwood had convinced her to vote Communist in the last election, she was now "talking reverently about 'The Führer.'" Nineteen years later, Isherwood returned to Berlin and paid a visit to a very surprised Frl. Thurau, who was now in her seventies and still living at Nollendorfstrasse 17 in a smaller flat.

Frl. Schneider is a supporting role in the play and film versions of *I Am a Camera*, yet she is one of the lead characters in the stage musical, *Cabaret*, which focuses on two couples: Sally Bowles and Clifford Bradshaw, and Frl. Schneider and Herr Schultz, a Jewish store owner who does not appear in Isherwood's novel. When Herr Schultz proposes to Frl. Schneider, she accepts and then realizes that if she

Comparison of Characters in *Goodbye to Berlin*, *I Am a Camera*, and *Cabaret*

Goodbye to Berlin Characters	Real person on whom character is based	*I Am a Camera* (1951, play)
Sally Bowles (UK)	Jean Ross	Sally Bowles (UK) (Julie Harris)
Christopher Isherwood (UK)	Christopher Isherwood	Christopher Isherwood (UK) (William Prince)
Fraulein Schroeder (Ger)	Meta Thurau	Fraulein Schneider (Ger) (Olga Fabian)
Fritz Wendel (Ger)	Franz von Ullman	Fritz Wendel (Ger) (Martin Brooks)
Natalia Landauer (Ger)	Gisa Soloweitschik	Natalia Landauer (Ger) (Marian Winters)
Clive (U.S.)		Clive Mortimer (U.S.) (Edward Andrews)

Name of actor who originated the role on stage or appears in the film and the character's nationality are in parentheses.

marries a Jewish man she risks losing her license to run her boardinghouse. In the end, she is forced to sacrifice her happiness and decline his proposal.

In the screenplay of *Cabaret*, screenwriter Jay Allen removed the Schneider/Schultz plotline and replaced it with the secondary plotline from John Van Druten's play, *I Am a Camera*, involving two characters from *Goodbye to Berlin* who never actually meet: Fritz Wendel, a gigolo, and Natalia Landauer, the young daughter of a wealthy Jewish

I Am a Camera **(1955, film)**	*Cabaret* **(1966, musical)**	*Cabaret* **(1972, film)**
Sally Bowles (UK) (Julie Harris)	Sally Bowles (UK) (Jill Haworth)	Sally Bowles (U.S.) (Liza Minnelli)
Christopher Isherwood (UK) (Laurence Harvey)	Clifford Bradshaw (U.S.) (Bert Convy)	Brian Roberts (UK) (Michael York)
Fraulein Schneider (Ger) (Lea Seidl)	Fraulein Schneider (Ger) (Lotte Lenya)	Fraulein Schneider (Ger) (Elisabeth Neumann-Viertel)
Fritz Wendel (Ger) (Anton Diffring)		Fritz Wendel (Ger) (Fritz Wepper)
Natalia Landauer (Ger) (Shelley Winters)		Natalia Landauer (Ger) (Marisa Berenson)
Clive (U.S.) (Ron Randell)		Maximilian von Heune (Ger) (Helmut Griem)

German department store owner. In the film *Cabaret*, Fritz pursues Natalia and her family's money, only to discover that he has actually fallen in love with her. Natalia tries to resist his advances because her family insists she marry a Jew, thereby forcing Fritz to reluctantly "come out" as Jewish.

The character of Fritz Wendel is modeled after Hungarian businessman Franz von Ullmann. According to Isherwood's friend, British poet Stephen Spender, von Ullmann was Jewish and a baron, but that was not his real last name and he was a homosexual "fond of tawny lads." Von Ullmann also introduced aspiring actress Jean Ross to Isherwood and Spender. Wendel also appears, along with Frl. Schroeder, in Isherwood's other Berlin novel, *Mr. Norris Changes Trains*, which tells the story of Christopher's friendship with Mr. Norris, an enigmatic and ultimately less than honorable gentleman.

Christopher's pupil, Natalia Landauer, who is the subject of the story "The Landauers," is based on Gisa Soloweitschik, the daughter of a Lithuanian Jewish banker whom Isherwood met through Spender. Isherwood remembers Gisa as a genuinely warm person, very different from the uptight, prudish Natalia, who was conceived as the polar opposite of the outrageous Sally Bowles. Natalia's father was loosely based on Wilfrid Israel, the Anglo-German Jewish owner of one the largest department stores in Berlin. Once the war broke out, Israel moved to England, where he tried to help Jews get out of Europe. He died when a carrier plane flying back from Portugal was shot down over the Bay of Biscay by the Germans. Among the casualties was actor Leslie Howard (*Gone with the Wind*), who is believed to have been working as a spy for British intelligence.

I Am a Camera (1951/play, 1955/film)

> I am a camera with its shutter open, quite passive, recording,
> not thinking. . . . Some day, all this will have to be developed,
> carefully printed, fixed.

The above passage from the opening of *Goodbye to Berlin*
begins with the oft-quoted phrase for which Isherwood is
best known: "I am a camera." Christopher, who has just arrived in Berlin, is sitting at the window of his room watching and listening to the sights and sounds of the city street
below. Isherwood claims the camera was intended to be a
metaphor for how Christopher, as a "detached foreign visitor," was feeling at that moment. Unfortunately, the metaphor was repeatedly taken out of context by critics in their
assessment of Isherwood's writing style, which was praised
for his "sharp camera eye" and criticized for his cameralike
emotional detachment from his characters.

The phrase was immortalized by playwright John Van
Druten, who chose it for the title of his 1951 stage adaptation of *The Berlin Stories*. Like Isherwood, Van Druten was
an English expatriate who enjoyed a successful career in the
London theater before moving to New York, where he wrote
such Broadway hits as *I Remember Mama* (1941) and *The*

Voice of the Turtle (1943). His decision to adapt Isherwood's stories was supposedly sparked by a remark made by Dodie Smith, a mutual friend of Isherwood's and author of the novel *The One Hundred and One Dalmatians* (1956). With the intention of planting the idea in the playwright's head, Smith said it would be impossible to turn *The Berlin Stories* into a play. By the next day, Van Druten announced that he had completed outlining the first half of the play, which incorporated a plotline directly from the second story in *Goodbye to Berlin*, "Sally Bowles," involving Sally and Christopher's friendship with a rich, brash American named Clive.

The structure of Van Druten's adaptation is very much in the spirit of Isherwood's novel because unlike most three-act plays, it comprises a series of loosely connected incidents (Sally's relationship with roommate Christopher, her abortion, their friendship with Clive, etc.) that occur over a four-month period. As in the novel, Sally deliberately hurts Christopher's feelings by criticizing his writing, which puts a strain on their friendship. Van Druten then introduces a new character who does not appear in Isherwood's novel: Sally's mother, Mrs. Watson-Courtneidge. She disapproves of her daughter's lifestyle and travels to Berlin to take her home. It appears that bohemian Sally is going to give in to her mother's demands until she tricks her into returning to England without her. Isherwood's favorite moment in the play is in the final scene, when the audience is led to believe that a defeated Sally, dressed in a "frumpy, respectable, middle-class coat," is returning to England, only to see her take off the coat and reveal "a sort of bohemian uniform, a tight-fitting black silk dress with a flaming scarf," meaning the "squares are defeated, [and] the establishment has gone." The play ends with Christopher and Sally confessing they are fond of each other. She turns down his offer to come home with him and decides to run off instead with a Yugoslavian film producer.

Van Druten, who was clearly aware of how the critics might respond to his plotless adaptation, wrote a piece for the *New York Times* before the reviews even came out, defending *I Am a Camera* as a "mood play." Citing Chekhov and Ibsen as his major influences, Van Druten admits plots are not his strong point and he doesn't write "message plays": "My aim was that the whole thing became one portrait," he explains, "of the life in Berlin in 1930 and of the handful of people selected as its protagonists." In his introduction to the published edition of *I Am a Camera*, Van Druten notes that his play is plotless, but he doesn't consider the ending—in which Christopher and Sally realize they love each other but it's not enough to hold them together—to be pointless, only untraditional because no one dies or gets married. Unfortunately, the play's shortcomings, particularly its lack of a plot, did not elude critics, who characterized *Camera* as "a play that has no center" (*Time*), "a little obvious and immature" (the *New Yorker*), and "never . . . dull, [yet] it never accomplishes much" (*New York Times*). Then, of course, there is the famous three-word review—one of the shortest on record—by Walter Kerr for the *New York Herald*, "Me no Leica" (a Leica is a German camera). Despite Kerr's review, the play received the New York Drama Critics Circle award and ran for a total of 214 performances.

The play's popularity and moderate run on Broadway can be attributed to its leading lady, twenty-six-year-old Julie Harris, who had achieved stardom overnight with her portrayal of Frankie Adams, a twelve-year-old tomboy, in the 1950 stage version of Carson McCullers' *The Member of the Wedding*. Although the critics may have had trouble with the play, they had nothing but praise for Harris' "brilliant performance" (the *New Yorker*) as Bowles, whom she played "with amazing verve, and with a naughty-child air" (*Time*), and "a virtuosity and an honesty that are altogether stunning and that renew an old impression that Miss Harris has the quicksilver and the genius we all long to discover on the stage" (*New York Times*). For her performance, Harris received her first of five Tony Awards (in 2002 she received her sixth for Special Lifetime Achievement).

Attributing the play's success to Harris, Isherwood felt he first understood his own character when Harris brought a

Joan of Arc, militant bohemian quality to the role. Isherwood recalled discussing with Van Druten the possibility that Sally's sex life is completely imaginary, and leaving it up to the audience to decide. In other words, Sally is not really a "tart," but a little girl who is copying what grown-ups have said about tarts. Harris also saw her as a "sad, child-like creature" who behaves in "an outrageous way because she wanted to be noticed."

Harris repeated her role in the 1955 film version costarring Laurence Harvey in the Isherwood role and Shelley Winters as Natalia Landauer. Both Isherwood and Van Druten passed on penning the screenplay, which was written by British author John Collier and directed by Henry Cornelius, who was best known for the popular British comedy *Genevieve* (1953). Expanding the action of the play beyond the walls of Fraulein Schneider's flat gives the audience a taste of prewar Berlin (even if it looks like a studio back lot), including the cabaret where Fritz takes Christopher to watch Sally Bowles perform. Donning a black-sequined skirt with a slit up the middle and a matching tuxedo jacket and bow tie à la Marlene Dietrich, she sings "I Only Saw Him in a Cafe in Berlin," a tune based on a 1951 German song popularized by Dietrich ("Ich Hab Noch Einen Koffer in Berlin" ["I Have Another Suitcase in Berlin"]) with new English lyrics.

I Am a Camera ran into some difficulty with the "censors" in the United States, which ultimately limited its release in theaters. The Production Code Administration (PCA) "regulated" film content in the United States in accordance with the Hollywood Production Code, a list of restrictions on profanity, the treatment of adult themes, and the depiction of violence, sex, and nudity. *I Am a Camera* was denied a Certificate of Approval because it dealt with the subject of abortion and "gross promiscuity on the part of the leading lady [Bowles] without proper compensating moral values." The distributor's appeal was denied, even when changes were made in the Code in 1956 to allow the treatment of "certain subjects" (abortion, drug addiction, kidnapping of children) "under conditions which assure restrained and careful treatment." *I Am a Camera* still failed to meet the requirements because the subject of abortion is treated lightly and not condemned. Ironically, Sally doesn't even have an abortion in the film because unlike in the play, she discovers she's not pregnant after all. The film was also condemned by the Catholic Legion of Decency on the grounds that "the film in basic story, characterization, dialogue and costuming offends Christian and traditional standards of morality and decency and must, therefore, be judged as wholly unsuitable for all persons, youth and adults." Still, *I Am a Camera* was shown at independently owned theaters in major markets like Los Angeles and New York, and in smaller cities around the country.

Once again, the critics had nice things to say about Harris, who received a British Academy Award nomination (for Best Foreign Actress) for her performance, but dismissed the film as, to quote the *New York Times*' Bosley Crowther, "meretricious, insensitive, superficial, and just plain cheap." Instead of delving deeper into the social and political aspects of Berlin life in the 1930s, the filmmakers chose to go for cheap laughs with an overlong farcical sequence in which Sally and Clive (Ron Randell), the American millionaire, try to cure Chris (Laurence Harvey) of his hangover in the middle of an outlandish party by subjecting him to a series of extreme and painful treatments. Consequently, the subplot involving Fritz (Anton Diffring) and Natalia (Shelley Winters), which would be artfully woven into the film *Cabaret*, fades into the background. In addition, the story is actually told in flashback by an older Chris, now a successful author living in London. He reluctantly attends a party given by a publisher for a new book, *The Lady Goes on Hoping*, and is shocked to discover that the author is none other than Sally Bowles, who once again talks Christopher into letting her stay at his place.

Sally Bowles made a good first impression on the stage and screen. One decade later, she would be reincarnated— and set to music.

CHAPTER 3

The idea of turning Isherwood's Berlin stories into a stage musical is attributed to Harold Prince, whose producing credits included such critical and commercial Broadway hits as *The Pajama Game*, *Damn Yankees*, *West Side Story* (1957), and *Fiddler on the Roof* (1964). While Prince was in the early stages of developing the project, English composer/lyricist Sandy Wilson, best known for his Roaring '20s musical, *The Boy Friend* (1953), which introduced American audiences to Julie Andrews, was commissioned by producer David Black to adapt Van Druten's *I Am a Camera* as a vehicle for Andrews. Once Prince secured the rights, which put an end to Black's project, Prince listened to Wilson's score, but passed on it because it didn't "fit in with his conception of Sally Bowles."

Joseph Masteroff, who wrote the book for another Prince musical, *She Loves Me* (1963), was already involved in the project when Prince asked composer John Kander and lyricist Fred Ebb to write the score. Prince had produced Kander and Ebb's short-lived musical, *Flora, the Red Menace*, starring nineteen-year-old Liza Minnelli. Kander and Ebb wrote *Cabaret* with Minnelli in mind, but Prince thought she was too good of a singer and wanted Sally to be British and the Christopher character (renamed Cliff Bradshaw) to be American. Minnelli recalls that when she, Kander, and Ebb first heard the idea of making a musical about pre-Nazi Germany, they wondered, "What are we going to call it? *The Nifty Nazi Follies*?" Minnelli was disappointed she wasn't cast as Sally Bowles, yet she somehow knew that she would one day do the movie.

In his autobiography, *Contradictions: Notes on Twenty-Six Years in the Theatre*, Prince explained it wasn't the character of Sally Bowles that attracted him to the material, but the parallels he saw between the "spiritual bankruptcy" of Germany in the 1920s and racism in America in the 1960s. To illustrate his point, on the first day of rehearsal Prince brought a photo of a group of young, shirtless, Aryan-looking demonstrators angrily looking into the camera. Everyone assumed it had been taken in Germany in 1929, but it was actually shot by *Life* photographer Norris McNamara at a recent protest against integration at a Chicago school.

Set in Germany in 1929–30, the plot of *Cabaret* focuses on two couples: Sally Bowles (Jill Haworth), a British cabaret singer, and Cliff Bradshaw (Bert Convy), an American writer, and an older couple, Cliff's landlady, Fraulein Schneider (Lotte Lenya), and another tenant, Herr Schultz (Jack Gilford), a kindly Jewish fruit seller. The stage musical opens with Cliff traveling on a train to Berlin, where he meets and befriends Ernst (Edward Winter), a German who refers him to Fraulein Schneider's boardinghouse. That evening, New Year's Eve, 1930, Cliff meets Sally after watching her perform at the Kit Kat Klub. On the following morning, she arrives at his room with her suitcases, claiming her jealous boyfriend kicked her out and she needs a place to live. Cliff reluctantly agrees to let her move in. The pair fall in love; Sally becomes pregnant and accepts Cliff's proposal of marriage. To make money to support his family, Cliff abandons his writing and accepts a temporary job as a courier for Ernst, who, unbeknown to Cliff, is a member of the Nazi Party.

Meanwhile, Frl. Schneider entertains and accepts a marriage proposal from Herr Schultz. At their engagement party, Ernst warns Frl. Schneider against this because in the changing political climate she risks losing everything being married to a Jew. In the end, both women come to a decision. Fearing she will lose her license to run her boardinghouse, Frl. Schneider declines Herr Schultz's proposal. Sally, unwilling to abandon her career to be a wife and mother, has an abortion without Cliff's knowledge and decides not to accompany him back to America. Leaving Berlin and Sally behind, he begins writing his novel about his experiences.

The creators of *Cabaret* succeeded in transforming Van Druten's three-act character study into a darker, more theatrical commentary on the downward moral spiral of pre-Nazi Germany. The cabaret where Sally performs, the Kit Kat Klub, is a temporary haven from the social realities and political turmoil of the outside world. Presiding over the onstage festivities is a painted-faced Emcee (Joel Grey), a crude, clownish figure who is the embodiment of decadent Berlin. Prince initially struggled with the conception of the musical, which was at first more conventional, with the Emcee and others coming out in the beginning and performing a six-minute set of songs about life in Berlin that imitated performers of the period. While vacationing in Russia, Prince saw the Taganka Theatre's production of *Ten Days That Shook the World*, a political revue loosely based on John Reed's eyewitness account of the 1917 Russian Revolution. Prince considers the experience a "turning point" in his "thinking as a director." The production's innovative staging and use of space to capitalize "on the special relationship between the live actors and the live observers" inspired Prince's staging of *Cabaret*, for which he divided the stage into two general areas:

> I suggested splitting the stage in two: an area to represent the REAL WORLD, the vestibule in Sally's rooming house, her bedroom, the train, the cabaret; and an area to represent the MIND. Joel Grey's material was divided between realistic numbers performed in the cabaret for an audience on stage and metaphorical numbers illustrating changes in the German mind. We call this the Limbo Area. . . . At the climax of the show, Sally Bowles sang "Cabaret," lost track of her audience, broke down, and for the first time in the evening, stepped across the footlights into the Limbo Area, and the audience understood.

Scenic designer Boris Aronson also hung a large, slanted mirror above the center of the stage that reflected the audience, which "cast an additional, uneasy metaphor over the evening."

The songs sung in the "real world," typical of those found in the traditional "integrated" musical, forward the plot and develop the characters: the Emcee (Joel Grey) welcomes us to the Kit Kat Klub ("Willkommen"), Sally's naughty nature is revealed to Cliff ("Don't Tell Mama"), and she convinces him to let her move in ("Perfectly Marvelous"), Herr Schultz and Frl. Schneider reflect on the virtues of getting married ("Married"), etc. The "metaphorical numbers," which are characteristic of what is now commonly referred to as a "conceptual musical," are the Emcee's songs that serve as commentary on the times. When Sally invites herself to move in with Cliff, the Emcee, with a woman on either side, launches into "Two Ladies," a comical homage to a *ménage à trois*. In act 2, Fraulein Schneider shares her fears about what could happen if she were to marry Herr Schultz and the Nazis come to power. The emotional scene is followed by the song, "If You Could See Her (The Gorilla Song)," in which the Emcee pleads for tolerance for himself and his true love—a female gorilla in a pink tutu.

The song is quite comical—until the last line: "And if you could see her through my eyes, she wouldn't look *Jewish* at all." At that point, the audience realizes that the song, as performed in the context of the show, is not trying to teach the patrons of the Kit Kat Klub a moral lesson but pandering to the growing anti-Semitism in Germany. Fred Ebb, who said the song came to him in a dream, later explained he was trying "to show how anti-Semitism was creeping in." Unfortunately, everyone did not see it that way. During the Boston tryout and then in New York, the producers received letters from Jewish activists protesting that the song was anti-Semitic (ironically, Prince, Kander, and Ebb are all Jewish). Bowing to the pressure of a boycott, Prince had Ebb change the line to "she wouldn't be a *meeskite* at all." *Meeskite* is a Yiddish word for an ugly person, and the title of a song performed by Herr Schultz in an earlier scene that teaches a moral lesson about looking beyond the surface and loving someone for who they are ("Though you are not a beauty it is nevertheless quite true/There may be beautiful things in you"). The original line ("she wouldn't look Jewish at all") was occasionally thrown in by Joel Grey and later used in the film, though it was shot without music in case there was a negative reaction and the line had to be re-recorded.

Fred Ebb estimated that he and John Kander wrote a total of forty-seven songs for *Cabaret*; fifteen are in the final version of the show, and six of those fifteen are in the film version. Kander listened to German jazz and vaudeville songs, though he admitted years later that, as he does with all shows, he put them out of his mind while composing. In trying to write music in the style of the period, Kander knew some critics would accuse him of ripping off Kurt Weill, Germany's leading composer of that era and the late ex-husband of cast member Lotte Lenya. When Kander explained to Lenya, whom he considered "the conscience of *Cabaret*," that he never intended to copy Weill, she took his head in her hands and said, "No, no, it's not Kurt. When I'm onstage, it's Berlin that I hear when I sing your songs."

The participation of Lotte Lenya certainly added an air of authenticity to the musical. As Masteroff observed, "When she walks onstage she brings it all with her." Joel Grey, who describes Lenya as a "very, very, feisty, interesting woman," says to ensure he was being authentic, he was "always going to her and saying 'Am I right? Is this right?'" Lenya's career started in Berlin in the late 1920s when she created the role of Jenny in the original 1928 production of *The Threepenny Opera*, written by Weill and Bertolt Brecht. She repeated the role in the 1931 German film directed by G. W. Pabst and again over twenty years later in the 1954 Broadway revival, for which she won a Tony. Considering her roots, it's not surprising that Lenya was not a fan of the traditional, integrated musical, going as far as to say that "the worst thing that ever happened to the American musical was 'Oklahoma!'"

The roles for Grey, Lenya, and Jack Gilford were written specifically for them, leaving Prince and his collaborators the task of casting the role of Sally. According to one columnist, Prince had meetings with Joey Heatherton and actress Mia Farrow about playing Sally. In the end, he chose British actress Jill Haworth, who had appeared in three high-profile films directed by Otto Preminger, *Exodus* (1960), *The Cardinal* (1963), and *In Harm's Way* (1965), but had no musical theater training. Grey thinks using the actress was an "interesting exercise for Hal [Prince]. He really did choose someone who was very much like the character. But there is a difference between acting and being." Masteroff recalls how Harold Prince assured his collaborators during the tryout in Boston prior to the New York opening that the success of the show was not going to rest on "how well her character registered." Unlike the film, the stage musical was not conceived as a star vehicle. In fact, in the show Sally only sings two and a half numbers ("Don't Tell Mama," "Cabaret," and the duet "Perfectly Marvelous"). Minnelli's Sally has three solos ("Mein Herr," "Maybe This Time," and "Cabaret," and a duet with the Emcee, "Money, Money").

Haworth, who was twenty when she was cast as Bowles, later admitted that the role was challenging for her: "I didn't like Sally at first—I didn't understand her. It was a difficult part, so many fragmented scenes. On the pre-Broadway tour they kept changing them and it confused me. When we settled down, things got better. She became more me. I was 20, full of life and crazy things, living for the moment." Judi Dench, who played the part in the 1968 London stage production, was familiar with Isherwood and *I Am a Camera*, which she admitted to having seen five times as a student: "I remember Sally completely clearly now. Very English, with nicotine-stained nails. They told me it didn't matter if I had no voice at all, because if the girl was crying underneath, she couldn't get the note either, and it was more truthful than if I were singing a perfect song."

Cabaret opened in New York at the Imperial Theatre on November 20, 1966, to reviews ranging from positive to mixed. Most critics found the musical entertaining and inventive, praising Kander and Ebb's score, Ron Field's musical staging, Boris Aronson's scenery, and the performances of Grey, Lenya, and Gilford. There was a consensus that the one major problem with the show was the casting of Jill Haworth. The most influential critic at the time, Walter Kerr of the *New York Times*, offered the harshest critique of her talents and performance: "She is trim but neutral, a profile rather than a person, and given the difficult things 'Cabaret' is trying to do, she is a damaging presence, worth no more to the show than her weight in mascara." In Kerr's mind, the culprit was really Prince, who, in casting Bowles, showed "a totally uncharacteristic lapse of judgment."

In the end, Prince was proven right. Haworth's limitations did not keep the theatergoers away. *Cabaret* ran for nearly three years (1,165 performances) and showed a profit of $1,350,000. The show was nominated for 10 Tony Awards and took home eight, including Best Musical, Direction, Costume Design (Patricia Zipprodt), Scenic Design, Choreography, Score, Featured Actor (Grey), and Featured Actress

(Peg Murray, who portrayed the prostitute living in Frl. Schneider's boardinghouse). Lenya lost to Barbara Harris in *The Apple Tree* and Gilford to Robert Preston in *I Do! I Do!*.

The Kit Kat Klub Goes Hollywood

While the Kit Kat Klub was still open for business on Broadway, the movie rights to *Cabaret* were on the auction block. In the summer of 1968, *Variety* reported that Cinerama Releasing Corporation, a distribution company, acquired the rights to *Cabaret* for $2.1 million. Seven months later, Cinerama pulled out, reportedly due to "escalating percentages" and interference from the six lawyers involved in making the deal. Kander, Ebb, and Masteroff filed a breach-of-contract suit against the company, which, in turn, claimed it had only made a verbal agreement to purchase the rights. The lawsuit was eventually settled out of court.

The rights to *Cabaret* were purchased in May 1969 for a considerably lower price, $1.5 million, by Allied Artists, an American distributor of exploitation films and foreign "art films." The company originally planned to produce the film in conjunction with Haven Industries but soon bought out their share. In January 1970, Allied struck a deal with ABC Pictures, the theatrical division of the American Broadcasting Company. With a budget of approximately $5 million, relatively low for a musical, ABC would produce the film and

Allied Artists would distribute it. ABC Pictures President Martin Baum told *Variety* he was confident a major musical could be made for that price if they "control costs and plan carefully." "We have *Song of Norway*," he added, "which was shot on location in 75 mm, coming in at $3.5 million." Unfortunately for ABC Pictures, when the film version of the 1944 operetta about the life of Edvard Grieg landed in theaters later that year, it was critically panned and a box-office flop.

To produce *Cabaret*, Baum hired veteran Broadway producer Cy Feuer, who was responsible for such hits as *Guys and Dolls* (1950), *Can-Can* (1953), and *How to Succeed in Business Without Really Trying*. Feuer had also directed such memorable musicals as *The Boy Friend* (after firing the original director, Vida Hope), *Silk Stockings* (1955), and *Little Me* (1962). Although he had never produced a film, Feuer worked in Hollywood as a composer and as head of Republic Pictures' music department. Between 1939 and 1942 he received a total of five Academy Award nominations (two in one year) for Best Score.

Hoping to expand into film producing, Feuer initially approached Baum with a script entitled *The Kicking Rabbi*, a vehicle for comedian Buddy Hackett, who would play a rabbinical student with hidden talent as a place kicker who is signed by the New York Giants. Fortunately, Feuer accepted Baum's offer to produce *Cabaret* instead. He traveled to Seattle to see a road company of the musical, which only confirmed the problems he'd had with the show when he saw it the first time in New York. As Feuer later explained in his autobiography, *I've Got the Show Right Here*, "the entire secondary story—that soupy, sentimental, idiotic business with the little old Jewish man [Herr Schultz] courting Sally's landlady [Fraulein Schneider] by bringing her a pineapple every day [actually it was only *one* pineapple]—had to be thrown out. I couldn't stand it. Besides, it was dull and uninteresting." He told Baum he would do it if he could throw out the pineapples and "put in a decent secondary love story—something that could appeal to young people."

To pen the screenplay, Feuer hired Jay Allen (also known professionally as Jay Presson Allen; the Jay is short for Jacqueline), a playwright and screenwriter known for her smart adaptations. Allen's screen credits included Alfred Hitchcock's *Marnie* (1964) and *The Prime of Miss Jean Brodie* (1969), which she adapted from her 1966 play based on the novel by Muriel Spark. Allen was the ideal writer for the project because the screenplay for *Cabaret* would require her to draw from three literary sources: Joe Masteroff's book for the stage musical; Van Druten's play, *I Am a Camera*, on which the musical was partly based; and Isherwood's Berlin stories.

In addition, Feuer and Allen agreed to three significant changes to the stage musical. First, the Fraulein

Schneider–Herr Schultz plotline would be replaced by the secondary love story from Van Druten's play involving Natalia Landauer, the Jewish department store heiress, and Fritz Wendel, the gigolo who falls for Natalia and is forced to admit he's Jewish in order to marry her. Herr Schultz and his pineapple were gone, but Frl. Schneider would remain, though her role would be reduced significantly over time. Second, the film would address the issue all three literary sources (including Isherwood's stories) avoided: the sexuality of the Christopher character, whose name was now Brian Roberts. He was once again British (Sally was now American) and, to borrow a phrase from Feuer, a "switch-hitter" (a slang term for a bisexual), which the producer believed added a twist to the main story.

The third change was the most radical because it involved a major convention of the musical genre. Feuer admittedly was not a fan of movie musicals in which people burst into song for no apparent reason. He decided to remove all of the songs from the stage musical that are sung outside of the Kit Kat Klub setting. "There can be no unjustified singing on the screen," he explained to Baum. "There's a reality about the movies that will not accept it. This is a show-business story and the singing takes place on the stage of the Kit Kat Klub. Period."

Director Bob Fosse shared their vision. He believed omitting the "book" songs was necessary to avoid making a movie musical that merely duplicated the Broadway show. As Fosse explained in an interview with *New York* magazine, "*Singin' in the Rain*, *An American in Paris*, all the Gene Kelly, Fred Astaire musicals—they're classics. But they represent another era. Today I get very antsy watching musicals in which people are singing as they walk down the street or hang out the laundry . . . in fact I think it looks a little silly. You can do it on the stage. The theatre has its own personality—it conveys a removed reality. The movies bring that reality closer."

Fosse's involvement in the project began in true Hollywood fashion—a lunch meeting with Cy Feuer. Fosse had heard from his friend Hal Prince that a film version of *Cabaret* was in the works. Liza Minnelli and Joel Grey had already been signed, but Feuer had still not hired a director. Feuer and Fosse's professional relationship dated back to 1961, when the producer hired Fosse to stage most of the musical numbers for *How to Succeed in Business Without Really Trying*. The following year, they collaborated again on the musical comedy *Little Me*, which won Fosse a Tony for his choreography.

Feuer had no doubt that Fosse was the right choice to direct *Cabaret* because the producer believed it was the eight musical numbers performed on the stage of the Kit Kat Klub that would make or break this movie. "As I saw it," Feuer later explained, "if one or two of the numbers didn't work, we had a flop. On the other hand, if all eight worked and the picture was a little short on dramatic direction, we could still have a hit. . . . I had to protect the musical numbers. And there is nobody better on musical numbers than Bob Fosse." Having been a dancer in burlesque houses at the age of sixteen, Fosse was also familiar with the seedy nightclub milieu. He was the ideal director for this project.

Although Feuer had every intention to hire Fosse, he was obligated to meet with some big-name directors about the project. Gene Kelly was interested, but his light sensibility was not a good match for such dark material. Billy Wilder turned it down because the subject hit too close to home. Wilder, who is Jewish, left Berlin when Hitler came to power, leaving behind his mother, stepfather, and grandmother, all of whom died at Auschwitz.

Fosse desperately wanted the job because he knew no one else would hire him after his first film, *Sweet Charity*, bombed at the box office. Based on the stage musical he conceived, directed, and choreographed, the film *Sweet Charity* had a $10 million price tag ($3 million over budget) and made only $4 million. Fosse and Universal Studios were surprised the film did so poorly because the initial reviews from the trade newspapers were generally positive. *Variety* called it a "terrific musical film . . . with sure fire entertainment values, stylishly and maturely planned and executed." The mainstream critics were less enthusiastic. Many of them praised his choreography, but most found the film, to borrow a phrase from *New York Times* reviewer Vincent Canby, "overly cinematic" and accused Fosse of relying far too heavily on cinematic tricks and fast-paced cutting. In an article that appeared in the *Times* four days later, Canby pointed out that *Charity* had the same problem as most other musicals of the period. Producers were all trying to make as much money as *The Sound of Music*, so they were unwilling to take risks, preferring adaptations of Broadway shows to original musicals.

Working closely with Feuer, and to a lesser extent Fosse, Jay Allen reworked the basic plot. The story focuses on the relationship between Brian (Michael York) and Sally (Liza Minnelli), who meet when he arrives in Berlin and moves into Fraulein Schneider's boardinghouse. He goes to watch Sally sing at the Kit Kat Klub, and the two become fast friends. Soon after, Sally makes a pass at Brian, who does not reciprocate, explaining that all of his sexual experiences with women have been disasters. They agree to be just friends. Meanwhile, Sally and Brian's friend, Fritz Wendel (Fritz Wepper), a self-admitted gigolo, begins to court one of Brian's English pupils, Natalia Landauer (Marisa Berenson), a prim and proper Jewish heiress. Fritz, who was initially interested in her because of the Landauer family fortune, fears he may actually be falling in love with her.

   One night, Sally returns home upset that her father broke their dinner date at the last minute. Brian comforts her, they kiss, and their friendship blossoms into a love affair. Their relationship is put to the test when the pair meet a very handsome and very wealthy German, Maximilian van Heune (Helmut Griem), who takes a liking to them both. He showers Sally with gifts and attention, which she accepts. Brian is cautious at first, but eventually warms up to him. When Sally accuses Brian of being jealous of Max, they quarrel and both admit they are sleeping with him. Max is soon out of the picture when at the last minute he changes his plans to take the couple to Africa. Sally and Brian's relationship is further complicated when she becomes pregnant. Brian offers to marry Sally and take her back to England with him.

   Natalia and Fritz's relationship also grows more complicated. He makes a pass at Natalia, who admits she has feelings for him, even though she knows he is a fortune hunter and they can never be married because he is not Jewish. Fritz realizes the only way he can be with Natalia is if he admits the truth—he is Jewish. The couple marry. But there is no wedding in the future for Sally and Brian, whose plans change when she decides to have an abortion behind his back. He says good-bye and returns to England, while she remains in Berlin to pursue her dream of becoming a star.

A closer look at the first draft of Jay Allen's screenplay (dated 6/10/70) reveals that decisions had been made early that all of the numbers, with the exception of "Tomorrow Belongs to Me," would be performed at the Kit Kat Klub. In addition, two of the Kit Kat Klub numbers—Sally's first song, "Don't Tell Mama," and the Emcee's "The Money Song (Sitting Pretty)"—are not included, but the script indicates new songs will be inserted. ("Mama" would be replaced by "Mein Herr" and "The Money Song" with the Sally–Emcee duet, "Money, Money"). An instrumental version of "The Money Song" can be heard on the soundtrack, along with a beautiful German rendition of the Frl. Schneider–Herr Schultz duet, "Married," sung by Austrian cabaret singer/actress Greta Keller, a contemporary of Marlene Dietrich known for her low singing voice. A third new song, "Maybe This Time," would also be added over the montage of Sally and Brian as they begin their love affair.

In September 1970, several months after the first draft of the script was completed, Allen, Fosse, and Feuer met with Allied Artists' chief executive, Manny Wolf, and his associates about the script. Feuer knew that Wolf was going to object to some of the dialogue, specifically the anti-Semitic comments made by some of the characters, so he made Allen and Fosse promise to stay calm. According to a memo summarizing the meeting from Cy Feuer to Wilfred E. Dodd,

President of Allied Artists, several issues related to the script were discussed, including the derogatory references to Jews, which Wolf and his colleagues wanted cut out. Feuer and her collaborators, of course, did not agree, but before the temperamental Fosse exploded, Allen spoke up and gave a heartfelt response to their request to essentially remove every occurrence of the word "Jew" from the script.

"I can certainly understand your feelings and I appreciate your sensibilities," she told them, "but look, I'm half Jewish myself, and I must tell you that I'd be profoundly offended if someone made a film about Berlin in the 1930s—and there was no mention of a Jew. And I can't think of any of my friends who wouldn't take to the barricades if that's the way this film was attacked. It's not a subject you can back out of."

In the end, all parties agreed to cut the expressions "Jew them down" and "Hollywood Jew," but keep "Jew producer" because Sally only says it to shock Natalia (Sally: "I spent all afternoon making love to an old Jew producer who's promised to give me a contract"). "Jew producer" was eventually cut as well. In the film, Sally instead uses the German word for fornication (*bumsen*) (Sally: "I spent the whole afternoon bumsening like mad with a ghastly old producer who's promised to give me a contract"). It was also agreed to keep Fritz's reference to Natalia as a "Jewess," but the line was changed in the final film to "The Landauers are enormous rich Jews."

Allen recalls that they left the meeting feeling "drained," and once outside, Feuer remarked, "Jay, I've been working with you for a year—and I didn't know you were Jewish." She replied, "Well, I'm not, but if you think I'm going into a meeting like that with an ethnic liability, you're crazy."

The first draft of the screenplay also introduces a new character, Sally's father, Mr. Bowles, who works for the American embassy in Rumania. When Brian reads in the paper that he is in town on business, Sally removes her green nail polish and puts on a demure dress and white gloves. She and Brian meet him for lunch, where her father embarrasses and belittles her. Sally claims that she has been working hard to learn German, yet she has a difficult time when he insists she demonstrate her language skills and order lunch for everyone at the table. He then scoffs at the notion that she will be a movie star ("It hardly is the face of a great actress," he says). Later that day, an angry Sally decides to let her father see that she is, as Brian observes, a "strange and extraordinary person." She changes into something more bohemian, puts her green nail polish back on, returns to her father's hotel, and waits for him in the lobby. When Mr. Bowles sees her, he is startled and disgusted by her appearance, tells her she looks like "some cheap little streetwalker," and orders her out of the hotel.

There were reservations expressed from the beginning about the inclusion of Mr. Bowles. Feuer's memo summarizing the script meeting notes at the bottom that Mr. Bowles is "somewhat one-dimensional and perhaps too heavy-handed. We agree to try to improve this character along these lines." Meanwhile, Fosse had given the script to his wife, Gwen Verdon, and two friends, playwright Neil Simon and television/screenwriter Robert Alan Aurthur, who would later collaborate with Fosse on the screenplay for *All That Jazz* (1979). They generally did not like the Mr. Bowles character and questioned why he was in the script. He was eventually eliminated and, in a far more powerful scene included in the final draft and in the film, Sally goes to meet him for dinner and after waiting for hours, returns home to find a telegram telling her that his schedule changed. She has a similar exchange with Brian about how no one loves her, which leads to their first kiss and the song "Maybe This Time."

"Maybe This Time" is the one Kander and Ebb song not written for the stage musical. It was a "trunk song" that had been recorded by eighteen-year-old Liza Minnelli on her first album, *Liza! Liza!*, released in 1964. She convinced Fosse to include the song, which perfectly expresses the hope that Sally, who gives the impression that she has slept with many men, may be feeling now that she and Brian are in love. As the song was not written for the film, it was ineligible for an Academy Award (the winner that year was "The Morning After" from *The Poseidon Adventure* [1972]).

In addition to Mr. Bowles, the other major change in the first draft of the script pertains to Brian's sexuality. In the original stage musical Christopher is heterosexual, while in *I Am a Camera* he seems to be almost devoid of any sexuality, though a line like "I'm not the marrying kind" certainly suggests that on the Kinsey Scale, with 0 being exclusively heterosexual and 6 exclusively homosexual, he would be closer to a 6 than a 0. As Jay Allen explained in the interview, "The idea of not playing the boy honestly and directly as a homosexual—as is the character in the book from which it all came—seemed antediluvian, dishonest." Brian Roberts is clearly not 100 percent homosexual, but seems to fall somewhere in the middle of the scale. In the original screenplay, the scene in which Sally makes a pass at him is much lighter in tone. When Brian says he doesn't sleep with girls, Sally apologizes and says, "It's so hard for Americans to tell with Englishmen. Whether they're queer or just well-bred." "The conditions do occasionally overlap," Brian replies. The word that best describes Brian is "bisexual"—someone who has a strong sexual attraction to both sexes. In 1972, Hollywood was still coming to terms with the subject of homosexuality, which in many ways was less challenging to depict than bisexuality because since the silent era homosexuals on the screen had been easily identified in a stereotypical fashion in terms of their dress, mannerisms, gestures, and speech.

But what does a male bisexual look like? How does he dress? Behave? The mutual sexual desire between Max and Brian is at last confirmed, albeit subtly, when they are alone in the *Biergarten* through an exchange of glances, a touch of their hands, and Brian's possession of a gold cigarette case—a gift from Max that he had refused to accept earlier in the film.

Kander and Ebb always had Minnelli in mind for Sally Bowles when they were writing the stage musical. Since Harold Prince had turned her down for the role, Minnelli's star continued to soar. She recorded four more albums and made television appearances, including headlining her own variety special, *Liza* (1970), written by Fred Ebb. Although she'd made her film debut at the age of three alongside her mother, Judy Garland, in the final scene of *In the Good Old Summertime* (1949), Liza's film career officially began in the late 1960s with a supporting role opposite Albert Finney in *Charlie Bubbles* (1967) and starring roles in *The Sterile Cuckoo* and *Tell Me That You Love Me, Junie Moon* (1970). Minnelli apparently considered her pre-*Cabaret* films her ticket to landing the role of Sally Bowles. In an interview given around the time of the film's release, she admitted, "I knew there would be a movie made from the play [*Cabaret*] and I wanted it. I decided I'd just have to have enough film credits by then to get the part." Feuer and Baum needed very little convincing, particularly after watching her perform the song "Cabaret" at the Olympia in Paris in December 1969. Liza recalled that they sent a note backstage after the performance: "If you sing it that way in the movie, you'll be the greatest Sally ever." Although he freely admits he can't take credit for the casting, Fosse had no doubts about Minnelli as Bowles. In an interview for *Penthouse*, he explained that he cast women who "I'd like to do it with, or if the part is an eighty-year-old washer-woman someone I'd like to have done it with when she was younger. She's got to have that attractive turn-on quality." That's exactly what he thought Liza had. "Even when I knew her as a kid," he adds. "It was brilliant casting. She's fantastic."

In addition to Kander and Ebb, Joel Grey was the only individual associated with the stage musical to be involved with the film. Since winning the Tony Award, Grey had starred as George M. Cohan in the Broadway musical, *George M!*, for which he received his second Tony nomination (a television version of the show was broadcast on NBC in September 1970). Grey was already signed to repeat the role of the Emcee when Bob Fosse was signed as director. Trying to distance the film from the stage show, Fosse was hesitant about having a member of the Broadway cast included. Baum and Feuer made the casting of Grey non-negotiable with Fosse, who, after meeting with Grey, thankfully agreed.

Michael York had heard they were looking for a "Michael York type" for the role of Brian Roberts, so he suggested to his agent that he might qualify. Other actors considered for the role included Murray Head, who played a bisexual in *Sunday Bloody Sunday* (1971), John Hurt, Ian McKellen, and Robin Askwith. Fosse later admitted that he and Martin Baum had to fight to get the guys writing the checks to approve York, whose credits included *The Taming of the Shrew* (1967), *Accident* (1967), *Romeo and Juliet* (1968), and the Hal Prince black comedy *Something for Everyone* (1970), in which he plays a conniving bisexual who beds a countess (played by Angela Lansbury) and her gay teenage son.

In mid-November, Fosse met with German actors for the other parts. The list of German actresses considered for the role of Natalia Landauer included several still working today in German television and cinema: Uschi Glas, Michaela May, Eleonore Weisgerber, and Gila von Weitershausen. Ironically, the role went to an American, Marisa Berenson, one of the fashion industry's highest paid models, who made her big-screen debut in Luchino Visconti's 1971 production of *Death in Venice*. She reportedly followed Fosse to London and Munich and was willing to do multiple screen tests. "I've never seen anyone so determined," he told an interviewer.

Two German actors were cast in the supporting male roles: Fritz Wepper (Fritz Wendel), who was known to

German television audiences as Harry Klein on *Der Kommissar* (1969–72) and later for the long-running police detective series, *Derrick* (1974–98); and Helmut Griem (Maximilian von Heune), who had played an SS officer trying to gain control of a family's steelmaking plant in *The Damned* (1969). In an interview with *After Dark*, Griem explained his take on the enigmatic bisexual baron:

> We are all bisexual by nature in that we have the capacity to be attracted to both men and women. I externalized those feelings, and attempted to project them through the character of the Baron. The Baron really liked both of them; perhaps he liked Brian a bit more. But the Baron was a catalyst in that he helped each of them see themselves more clearly and realistically before they parted.

The remaining cast members included six dancers, four Europeans and two Americans (Louise Quick and Kathryn Doby). Quick and Doby were "Fosse girls" who had appeared in both the stage and screen versions of *Sweet Charity* and would assist Fosse after *Cabaret* on the Broadway musical *Pippin* (1972). Quick was also the assistant choreographer on the Emmy-winning TV special, *Liza with a Z: A Concert for Television* (1972), while Doby had the same credit on Fosse's *All That Jazz* (1979), in which she was also featured.

Auditions were held in Germany for the other four dancers. Minnelli recalls, "It was funny because all the girls who came to audition for the roles of the dancers thought they were going to be in a Hollywood musical. Then they put the bruises on them and made them grow hair under their arms. They looked so confused at first." When they finished shooting the dance numbers, the cast had a party for them and gave them razors and soap so they could shave under their arms again.

One issue that became the source of great tension between Fosse the director and Feuer the producer was the director of photography. Fosse demanded they hire three-time Academy Award winner Robert Surtees, who had shot *Sweet Charity*. But to cut down on costs, Feuer and Baum wanted a European cinematographer. Whether Feuer did or did not promise to hire Surtees is not clear. In Munich, during preproduction on the film, Feuer received a telephone call from Martin Baum, who wanted to see how things were going. When Feuer said that the issue about the cinematographer had not been resolved, Baum suggested they just cut their losses and fire Fosse. Feuer assured Baum that Fosse was the right director for the project, yet he had no intention of hiring Surtees. In the hotel room next door, Fosse listened through the walls to Feuer's end of the conversation. The following morning, an angry Fosse confronted Feuer and accused him of lying and being duplicitous. Martin

Baum flew to Munich to referee. Fosse demanded that Feuer be fired, but Baum refused. Fosse and Feuer continued to work together on a professional basis, but their friendship was over. In a 1974 interview with *Penthouse*, the director explained that he can "live with ball-busting truth a lot easier than deception. That's what my differences with Cy Feuer were all about. I mean he lied to me. . . . If he'd leveled with me, we could have worked it out together. But he told me first one thing, then another. I can't stand deception."

Fosse did get Geoffrey Unsworth, the talented British cinematographer whose credits included such diverse films as *Othello* (1965), starring Laurence Olivier; the musical *Half a Sixpence* (1967); and *2001: A Space Odyssey* (1968). For his work on *Cabaret*, he would receive an Oscar, a British Academy Award, and a Best Cinematography award from the British Society of Cinematographers.

As for Kander and Ebb, they were not very involved in the project after contributing the three new songs. "We were told certain things were going to happen," Kander recalls. "A lot of people made decisions that nobody told us about. We didn't see anything until they showed us the rough cut." They received various drafts of the screenplay. "But I don't remember," Kander added, "anyone saying, 'Gee, what do you think?'"

CHAPTER 4

Shooting *Cabaret*
"A Most Strange and Extraordinary Journey"

Production on *Cabaret* began in Munich on February 22, 1971, with a six-week rehearsal period, approximately the same amount of time it takes to mount a Broadway show. The interior scenes, including the musical numbers performed in the Kit Kat Klub, were shot over several months at Bavaria Studios, located eight miles south of Munich. Founded in 1919, the historic studio has been the temporary home of some of Hollywood's top directors, including Alfred Hitchcock, Stanley Kubrick, John Huston, and Robert Wise. *Willy Wonka and the Chocolate Factory* (1971) had just wrapped production when *Cabaret* was moving in. The exterior scenes were filmed on location around Germany, including the streets of West Berlin and the lake district of Eutin, home of the baronial estate of the Duke of Oldenberg, which doubled as Maximilian's country estate.

Shooting in Germany and on location in West Berlin was integral to Fosse's vision of authenticity when it came to re-creating the sights and sounds of Berlin in the 1930s. In the production notes included in the film's press kit, Fosse admits, "I couldn't accept the usual Hollywood look of Berlin in the 30s. Consequently, we spent a great deal of time researching the period. We tried very hard for authenticity in our search for locations in Germany, and in everything we did."

As a visual director who paid very close attention to every detail, Fosse was extremely frustrated by the lack of research material on Berlin. He did receive some assistance from Germans who were there in the 1930s. In an interview with German avant-garde artist/critic Lil Picard for *Interview* magazine, Fosse explained, "I met a few people who were then patrons of the cabarets and cafes, but I never met any performers, and I found it very difficult to get into real research. Every time I tried to get any books in Germany, it was very difficult." Picard, who had worked as a journalist in Berlin in the '30s, responded that the Kit Kat Klub did not resemble the typical cabaret of the period, which she described as "a small intimate place with a strong political 'conferencier' that was the M.C." Picard insisted the type of entertainment performed onstage in the film was found in music halls, not cabarets. Fosse's response is very diplomatic: "Well, I have talked to more people about it . . . I think there is a great difference of opinion as to what exactly went on." When Picard asked why he didn't use any newsreel or archival footage, Fosse made his intentions very clear: "I was not out to make a factual film, a documentary. That was not the purpose of it. . . . I wanted to tell a love story, about human relationships."

Keeping It Authentic

When looking back at the making of *Cabaret*, one point members of the cast and crew seem to agree on is that Fosse knew what he wanted, and it carried over into every aspect of the production, right down to the smallest detail. "He had a vision and a point of view," Minnelli explains, "and that's what a director really needs. He was a perfectionist, and we went along with him." Dancer Louise Quick, who appeared in the stage and screen versions of *Sweet Charity*, remembers that when everyone arrived in Germany, Fosse was prepared: "Obviously he had done a great deal of pre-production work because when we went into rehearsals, he knew what he wanted. His attention to detail was always extraordinary. But for film it was intensified because there are close-ups. The rehearsal process was very intense." Once the film started shooting and the cast and crew saw the dailies (the raw, unedited footage screened one or two days later), they recognized that *Cabaret* was not going to be a typical Hollywood musical. "It felt like there was electricity in the air," Quick recalls, "because we knew *Cabaret* was going to be different and very special."

Shooting on location in Germany instead of a back lot in Burbank also fueled the creative energy of Fosse, his cast, and the crew and deepened the film's collaborative atmosphere. Fosse benefited the most, working 5,900 air miles away from the executives at Allied Artists and ABC Pictures, whose interference was minimal while he was shooting. Not that the "suits" in the front office didn't make their opinions known after watching the dailies. One day Fosse received a note from Hollywood complaining that the interiors of the Kit Kat Klub were too dark and smoky. "Fosse read the note aloud," Liza recalls, "and there was a long pause, and then a lot of ripping of paper."

Fosse worked closely with cinematographer Geoffrey Unsworth, production designer Rolf Zehetbauer, art director Hans Jürgen Kiebach, and set decorator Herbert Strabel to create the Kit Kat Klub's dark, smoky, claustrophobic interior. They had difficulty finding photographs of the cabarets of the 1920s, so they turned to artwork from the period for inspiration for the set decor and the lighting design, particularly the caricatures by Dadaist painter George Grosz (1893–1959) and the expressionistic paintings of Otto Dix (1891–1969). One of Dix's most famous paintings, *Portrait of the Journalist Sylvia von Harden* (1929), depicts the German journalist and poet sitting at a table in a cafe with a drink and her cigarette case in front of her. With a cigarette in her right hand and a monocle in her right eye, von Harden is a *Neue Frau* ("New Woman") of Weimar Berlin—a modern, independent woman who can sit alone without an escort in a cafe. Fosse re-created the painting, which can be seen the first time Fosse cuts away from the Emcee during "Willkommen."

In an effort to keep it authentic, Fosse avoided some of the common cinematic tricks used in movie musicals. He staged the musical numbers within the confines of the small stage, rather than making the space larger to accommodate the choreography. To capture the sound of the period, Fosse cut down the number of instruments and the size of the orchestra to eight to ten pieces, so the music sounded as if it was being played by the orchestra seen on the screen.

For Minnelli, research was a "nightmare" because Germans were so reluctant to talk about the 1930s. Minnelli did consult with Fosse as well as her father, director Vincente Minnelli, who introduced her to "all kinds of art and pictures of that era" that made her realize that "all women in the 1930s were not blonde and looked like Marlene Dietrich."

According to Minnelli, the original costumes created for her character posed a major problem because they "made me look like Joe Namath—wide Joan Crawford sleeves, padded shoulders, and pleats." Gwen Verdon came to the rescue and ventured to Paris to hunt down clothes in antique shops for both Minnelli and Berenson to wear. "The first ones [costumes] they made were just terrible," Berenson, granddaughter of fashion designer Elsa Schiaparelli, candidly admitted to *Interview* magazine, "so I threw a tantrum! She [Verdon] found things and I brought material from Paris."

For Grey, the challenge was to do a real German accent. Vic Heutschy, the film's publicist, said he remembers Grey walking around the set with a tape recorder rehearsing his lines. "My German had to be authentic in a global way," Grey explains, "so I worked with a German dialogue coach to talk in a specifically Berlin dialect. Now when I hear myself on the Broadway cast album, it sounds so American because people didn't do that authentic research for a musical."

Although working in Germany may have added a level of authenticity, the Americans also sensed a lack of trust among some of the Germans. After all, this was a film about a period in their recent history that they would all sooner forget. When Liza asked her driver questions about the past, "he got very defensive . . . and said haughtily, 'Hitler killed more Germans than anyone else!'"

LEFT: Jean Ross was writer Christopher Isherwood's inspiration for the character of Sally Bowles.

BELOW: The cast of the 1955 film *I Am a Camera* (left to right): Anton Diffring (Fritz Wendel), Julie Harris (Sally Bowles), Shelley Winters (Natalia Landauer), and Laurence Harvey (Christopher Isherwood).

ABOVE: "Leave your troubles outside!": Joel Grey and the Kit Kat Girls singing "Willkommen."

FACING: Liza Minnelli onstage at the Kit Kat Klub singing "Mein Herr."

Joel Grey strikes a pose as the Emcee.

Michael York as British writer Brian Roberts, a character loosely based on author Christopher Isherwood.

ABOVE AND FACING:
Sally Bowles (Liza Min-
nelli) and the Emcee
(Joel Grey) sing the joys
of "Money, Money."

RIGHT: A young Nazi
leads the patrons of a
biergarten in a rousing
rendition of "Tomorrow
Belongs to Me."

TOP: Fritz Wendel (Fritz Wepper) discusses his love life with his English tutor, Brian Roberts (Michael York).

BOTTOM: Natalia Landauer (Marisa Berenson) and Fritz Wendel (Fritz Wepper) on their wedding day.

Joel Grey had this sense from members of the film's crew. "They mistrusted how we were going to represent them and their story," he explains, "and [were afraid] that we were going to continue to blame Germany, even when their attitude was, 'we weren't even there.'" Minnelli recalls that some of the German actors who were excited to be in a Hollywood film didn't know what to think when the wardrobe staff dressed them in Nazi costumes: "They looked dismayed, thinking to themselves, 'This wasn't what we thought it was going to be.'"

The rise of National Socialism is foregrounded in both the stage musical and the film by the song "Tomorrow Belongs to Me." In the stage version, it is sung twice in act 1. The first time is onstage at the Kit Kat Klub by the waiters, who are joined by the Emcee. The second time is at Herr Schultz and Fraulein Schneider's engagement party by Fraulein Kost, a prostitute who lives in Frl. Schneider's building, who arrives uninvited with four sailors. Ernst arrives soon afterward and it is revealed to Cliff (and the audience) that he is a member of the Nazi Party. When Ernst realizes Herr Schultz is a Jew, he warns Fraulein Schneider not to marry him. As Ernst is about to leave, Fraulein Kost stops him and begins to sing. Ernst and the rest of the party guests—everyone except Fraulein Schneider, Herr Schultz, Cliff, and Sally—join in:

Oh, Fatherland, Fatherland, show us a sign
Your children have waited to see.
The morning will come when the world is mine,
Tomorrow belongs to me.

The song is disturbing for the audience, who, knowing where Germany is headed politically, immediately recognizes that what lies underneath this musical display of German nationalism is intolerance and anti-Semitism. But apparently everyone did not see the irony. Kander and Ebb received letters during the run of the show accusing them of writing a Nazi song. There were even people who claimed they'd heard it in Nazi Germany.

In the film, "Tomorrow Belongs to Me" is the only song performed outside of the Kit Kat Klub. On the car ride back to Berlin, Max and Brian stop at a biergarten and have a drink while Sally is sleeping in the car. The beginning of the scene is the pivotal moment because it's the first time it is suggested that there is something going on between the two men. Their attention suddenly shifts to an Aryan youth with an angelic face, who begins to sweetly sing "Tomorrow Belongs to Me." As the camera pans down, we see he is in a brown Nazi uniform with a swastika on his left arm. He is soon joined by two young waiters, other young men in Nazi uniforms, and customers of all ages who stand and sing along. The music begins to sound like a military march as it grows louder and the crowd sings with great fervor. Toward the end of the song, the Aryan youth makes a Nazi salute.

Vic Heutschy, the film's unit publicist, recalls that they ran into a problem with the extras when shooting the scene. "Some of the Germans thought we were doing something pro-Nazi and started heading for the exit. Wolfgang Glattes, the assistant director, who is from Germany, was very instrumental in stopping them and explaining that this film was anything but pro-Nazi." To prepare for the scene, Fosse asked the producers to hire an authority on the period to make sure the youth was doing the Nazi salute properly. But when it was time to shoot, four middle-aged German extras insisted he was doing it wrong. When they proceeded to show him how it's done, each of them did it differently. "Eventually, as I found out later," Fosse explained to *Interview* magazine, "there was one salute for the civilians and one for the military and there are several variations of the military one."

In the final shooting script, cowritten by Allen and Hugh Wheeler, who received the screen credit of "research consultant," "Tomorrow Belongs to Me" is actually sung twice. The first time is in an early sequence in the film, immediately after the scene in which Sally tries and fails to seduce Brian. The couple are sitting on a balustrade across from the fountain of the Charlottenburg Palace, the largest palace in Berlin, which dates back to the seventeenth century. They watch a boys' choir singing "Tomorrow Belongs to Me," which can then be heard in the background as Sally and Brian are walking. The scene ends with the two stopping to look at anti-Semitic graffiti painted on the wall, which Brian translates as: "Let Jewish blood spurt with the knife. Then we'll have a better life." Sally makes a face and suggests going to the movies.

As a director, Fosse knew what he wanted when it was time to shoot a scene, yet he was open to improvisation and suggestions from the actors. Michael York recalled that there was never any down time for the actors between shots. While the technicians were busy, "[Fosse] would improvise around the scene about to be filmed, often coming up with invaluable new insights that give further dimension to our characters. Invariably, by the time the set was ready he had brought us all to a creative boil." York found Fosse to be particularly helpful when he started studying the script and realized that compared to the other characters, who were extremely extroverted, Brian seemed like "cardboard." Fosse agreed there was something missing from his character, so rewrites were done on the set by Hugh Wheeler. The character of Brian became "very positive and playable."

Marisa Berenson was the cast member with the least acting experience. Her only film credit was Luchino Visconti's
Death in Venice (1971), in which she appeared in flashbacks
and had no dialogue. She said the difference between the
two directors was that Visconti was "old school" in the sense
that he "tells you what he wants in the beginning and gives
you the impression of not directing at all," while Fosse, a
member of the "new school," was an "incredible perfectionist. He knows exactly what he wants and shoots till he gets
it." Berenson's words ring true based on some of the tactics
he would use to get her in character or get a reaction out of
her. In a dramatic moment, Natalia is horrified when she
opens her front door and finds her dead dog lying on her
doorstep as Nazi youths are running away shouting "*Juden!*
Juden!" (Jew! Jew!). When Fosse couldn't get the reaction
he wanted, he had someone go to a local butcher and get
pieces of bloody meat, which he then put on the doorstep.
When she opened the door, her horrified reaction was all
the more real. To get her in character as the prim and proper
Natalia, Berenson said that Fosse would "whisper obscene
things into my ear and I would blush. He just loved getting
all of these reactions."

The four European dancers chosen to play Kit Kat Girls
had never done Fosse's work before. "They were scared
of him," Louise Quick explains, "and they had such great

respect and love for him." He also earned a reputation for being respectful of dancers during the audition process. "When he 'excused' people, he would not just say 'next,' but he went up to each one, looked them straight in the eye, [would] sometimes shake their hands, and [said], 'Thank you for coming.'" The phrase spread around Europe with dancers. If someone rejected you, the dancer would jokingly say, "Thank you for coming."

The extras appearing as the patrons of the Kit Kat Klub also adored Fosse because he treated them with respect. Publicist Vic Heutschy says that Fosse hated when Hollywood directors used the same extras in multiple scenes. Fosse and assistant director Wolfgang Glattes would go out hunting for German faces for the cabaret scenes. At the end of each day, the person in charge of extras casting would line up potential extras for Fosse to choose from for the next day. "He would go to each person and talk to them very gently," Heutschy explained. "When he turned someone down he wouldn't just say 'Sorry,' but he would tell them why."

The production kept a relatively low profile while shooting. Heutschy said Fosse understood the value of publicity and that it was a necessity, but he didn't like journalists visiting the set because he thought it distracted his actors. One welcomed visitor was legendary Hollywood director/ choreographer Busby Berkeley (*Gold Diggers of 1935* [1935],

Babes in Arms [1939]), who was being honored at the 1971 Berlin Film Festival. Heutschy arranged for Fosse and Minnelli to meet the seventy-five-year old Berkeley, who, like Fosse, had begun as a dance director on the Broadway stage and then started working as a film director/choreographer (Fosse had danced on television and in films before becoming a choreographer on Broadway, which he continued to do in between directing films).

Production wrapped on *Cabaret* on July 9, 1971, slightly over budget. Consequently, there were scenes that were not shot, including one dramatic sequence set in the Landauer Department Store. Natalia stands in a store window yelling at the Nazis, who are outside spray-painting "Juden" on the glass. They take a bike away from a man who is yelling at the Nazis and hurl it through the window. Fritz, who is part of the crowd outside, rushes to help Natalia, whose face is cut by the shattered glass. He punches two Nazis out and then tends to Natalia as the two gaze into each other's eyes. There is a cut to a synagogue, where, as in the film, the wedding ceremony is being performed for Natalia and Fritz.

Making the Film (in the Editing)

"A film is made in the editing" is a familiar credo in the film industry, though it is heard more often out of the mouths of overworked editors than from ego-driven directors who could never admit that their film was created (and in some instances saved) in postproduction.

Bob Fosse understood the art of editing. In his semiautobiographical musical, *All That Jazz* (1979), the audience witnesses director/choreographer Joe Gideon (Roy Scheider) going through the painstaking process of editing a sequence from his new film, *The Stand-up*, over and over in hope of getting it right.

David Bretherton, who won an Oscar for his work on *Cabaret*, characterized his working relationship with Fosse as collaborative, though it got off to a rocky start. While shooting the film, Fosse never communicated with his editor. When shooting was completed and the director arrived back in New York, he asked Bretherton if he could see all of the dailies. Unbeknown to him, Bretherton had already assembled the entire film. As Bretherton told the story, when Fosse saw it, he said, "Oh, God, I'm ill." The next day, Fosse returned and said, "Look, did I disturb you yesterday? I didn't mean to say that. I thought I was going to see all of the dailies." So the editor and director went through the film reel by reel. Fosse objected to the way Bretherton had cut the dance numbers in the Kit Kat Klub. "I told him that the script gave the feeling of a shlocky nightclub where the dancers are sweaty and not very good. I put the missteps in on purpose." Fosse told him to recut it and have all the chorus girls at the same height.

Bretherton recalled how Fosse spent most of the time outside the cutting-room door, pacing back and forth like a panther. Thinking it would save time to have Fosse in the room with him choosing which take to use, Bretherton kept inviting him in. Finally, one day, Fosse admitted that the reason he didn't come in and sit down was that he had the "worst case of hemorrhoids anyone ever had." "All of a sudden, all of the walls, all the noncommunication just dissolved," Bretherton said. "God, I loved that man. I respected him, but was afraid of him. When he told me that, he became human."

The editing style employed in *Cabaret*, especially in the dance sequences, is not characteristic of classical Hollywood films, in which editing is "invisible" in the sense that its central function is to preserve the continuity of space and time. As in the tradition of the European art cinema of the 1950s and 1960s (i.e., Jean Luc-Godard's *Breathless* [1959], Federico Fellini's *8½* [1963], Michelangelo Antonioni's *Blow-up* [1966]), and the New Hollywood Cinema movement that began in the late 1960s, the editing is not subordinate to the story but is used in a highly self-conscious manner to foreground the film's theme.

The dance sequences in Hollywood musicals traditionally use minimal editing in order to capture the dancers' full bodies in motion and the fluidity of their movements. But the dance sequences in *Cabaret* serve a thematic function: to comment on the changing political climate in Germany as the Nazis become a more visible and powerful force and to contrast social realities of the "real world" with the unreal, onstage decadence in the Kit Kat Klub, where the Emcee encourages the audience to "leave their troubles outside."

For example, the opening number, "Willkommen," starts with the Emcee looking directly into the camera (a highly self-reflexive moment) as he welcomes both audiences (the film audience and those seated within the club) to the Kit Kat Klub. The song continues as Fosse cuts away to shots of Brian Roberts arriving by train to the city. This style of cross-cutting is used for more dramatic (and chilling) effect during the comical Bavarian slap dance, which is intercut with the brutal beating of the owner of the Kit Kat Klub by three Nazis, one of whom he chased out of the club for soliciting money from the patrons. The *oom pah pah* music, the slapping, and the stomping of the feet drown out the sound of the real bloody punches being thrown outside as the pace quickens, with the shots becoming shorter and shorter. The one potential problem was the length of the slap dance, which originally lasted only twenty seconds. Fortunately, Fosse always shot with more than one camera, so by using different angles of the same film, Bretherton doubled the length of the dance and repeated parts of the music track.

A similar contrast is made through the cross-cutting of the Emcee in drag and the Kit Kat Girls doing the "Tiller Girls" number (so named after the popular 1900s British dance troupe known for their precision dancing) with the young Nazis leaving Natalia's dead dog on her doorstep. At the moment she discovers the dog, cabaret dancers transform themselves into soldiers and start goose-stepping around the stage. Credit for this effective use of editing should also be given to screenwriter Jay Allen, who, in the first draft of her screenplay, crosscuts between scenes in all of the sequences described above, with the exception of the "Tiller Girls."

A rough cut of the film was finally assembled and shown to Kander and Ebb, who were told beforehand that what they were seeing was not finished and to expect missing sounds and black lines across the screen. Ebb admitted that he tried, but he couldn't get past the roughness, and it wasn't until he had seen the final version a few times that he really started to appreciate Fosse's work.

One of the people who attended an early screening of the film was Minnelli's father, director Vincente Minnelli. When it was over, he turned to Bob Fosse and said, "I have just seen the perfect movie."

CHAPTER 5

"Life *Is* a Cabaret"

ABC Pictures and Allied Artists had a very good reason to be confident *Cabaret* would be a moneymaker before the first review hit the newsstands.

Before a film is released in theaters, Hollywood studios hold test screenings to find out what audiences like and don't like about it. After the screening, participants are asked to share their opinion by filling out a reaction card or participating in a group discussion facilitated by the studio's marketing department or an outside firm. In some instances, a majority opinion can affect a film's marketing campaign or even the film itself. *Fatal Attraction* (1987), *Pretty in Pink* (1986), and *Little Shop of Horrors* (1986) were all reshot based on test audiences' negative reactions to their original endings. The production numbers in

James Brooks' 1994 musical comedy about the film industry, *I'll Do Anything*, were cut out of the film based on the negative response they received from test audiences. Ironically, Julie Kavner's character in the film is a test-screening analyst.

This was not the case with *Cabaret* after test screenings were held in Anaheim, California; Westwood Village in Los Angeles; San Francisco; and Minneapolis prior to the film's release in February 1972. In all four locations, the film received an overwhelmingly positive response. Approximately 70 percent of the over 1,200 people who filled out response cards rated the film "excellent," 20 percent said it was "good," 6 percent rated it "fair," and 4 percent checked "poor." To say the film "tested well" is a gross understatement. These numbers are what every studio executive dreams about for an upcoming release.

The specific comments audience members made in response to two screenings in Westwood Village (on January 21 and 22, 1972) and one screening in Anaheim (on January 22), which can be found in the Bob Fosse and Gwen Verdon Collection in the Music Division of the Library of Congress, were fairly consistent in terms of likes and dislikes. Most people summed up their reactions in one word (plus an exclamation point) ("Great!" "Wonderful!" "Terrific!" "Superb!"), while others chose to qualify their response:

"The most enjoyable movie I've seen in a long time!"

"The best film musical I've ever seen."

"It is probably the best film adaptation of a play ever made."

"Not only one of the best musicals of any year, but one of the best movies of all time!"

Some respondents went as far as to say that *Cabaret* was superior to other recent movie musicals, such as *The Boy Friend* (1971) and *Fiddler on the Roof* (1971).

"*What did you like most about* Cabaret?" The number one response was "Liza," with "Joel Grey" coming in a close second, followed by "Michael York." Many people accurately predicted that both Liza and Grey would win Academy Awards for their performances. Fosse's direction did not go unrecognized, along with the cinematography and the production design. The one technical aspect of the film that many people felt could be improved was the editing, specifically the film's running time and overall pacing, though they couldn't agree on what exactly should be cut (number one answer: the scenes involving Fritz and Natalia).

The strongest negative critical reactions were from people who had seen or were familiar with the stage musical. In most instances, they objected to the changes, specifically the songs that were cut ("Don't Tell Mama" and "It Couldn't Please Me More [A Pineapple]") and the replacement of the Fraulein Schneider/Herr Schultz plotline with the Fritz/

Natalia story, which some people also felt ended too abruptly. Surprisingly, the other major change to the story, Brian's bisexuality, did not elicit many negative responses, except from audience members who attended the screening at Cinemaland II in Anaheim, located in the heart of conservative Orange County, California. They asked if making Brian a "queer" and a "sex deviant" was necessary. One respondent accused the filmmakers of turning a "lovely play" into a "degenerate movie" (an interesting and ironic choice of words considering that "degenerate" was used by the Nazis in their campaign against modern art).

For many respondents, what distinguished *Cabaret* from other movie musicals was its adult subject matter and themes (Nazis, anti-Semitism, bisexuality). Up to that time, musicals had been synonymous with family entertainment, so some audience members were compelled to remind the film's distributor that it was their responsibility to make clear in the marketing campaign that the film was not intended for a family audience. Many people objected to the use of profanity. Actually, it was the use of one profane word: "fuck." Some found it objectionable, though one person, who accurately predicted it would be edited out in the final version, actually made a passionate plea for its inclusion: "Please, *please* don't edit out any of the movie, esp. concerning the use of the word 'fuck.' It was appropriate, and I believe that scene, which is crucial to the movie, would lose its effectiveness if excised." The scene in question is the pivotal moment in the script in which Sally and Brian reveal to each other (and the audience) that they are sleeping with Maximilian:

> Brian: Oh, screw Maximilian!
> Sally: I do!
> Brian: So do I.

In the version of the film screened for test audiences, Brian says, "*fuck* Maximilian," which is how the line appears in the first draft of the script, instead of "*screw* Maximilian," which is how it reads in the final draft of the screenplay. Michael York recalled that he and Minnelli shot the scene a second time under protest, substituting the euphemism "screw." "Outraged by the request," York explained, "Liza and I determined to perform the bowdlerized version so badly it could never be used, forcing adherence to the original. Of course it was used and I still wince when I see it." Changing the word most likely made it possible for the film to get a PG rating ("Parental Guidance Suggested—Some material may not be suitable for pre-teens") instead of an R ("Restricted: Persons under 18 not admitted, unless accompanied by parent or adult guardian"), which would have limited the film's potential audience. Ironically, when ABC aired the film on television, the entire conversation was edited out, no doubt leaving many viewers who had not seen the film in theaters (including myself) wondering what exactly, if anything, was going on among Sally, Brian, and Max.

The world premiere of *Cabaret* was held in New York City on Saturday, February 13, 1972, at the Ziegfeld Theatre, where the film enjoyed a five-month "exclusive engagement." The premiere screening, followed by a benefit dinner at the Hilton hotel for the Police Athletic League, was attended by the cast members, Fosse, Feuer, Shirley MacLaine, and Desi Arnaz, whose son, Desi Arnaz Jr., was dating (and rumored to be engaged to) Liza. On the following Saturday evening, a local half-hour television special on the film and the premiere aired on WOR-TV in New York.

Also airing that week was a ninety-minute salute to *Cabaret* on *The David Frost Show* with Fosse and the cast, featuring musical performances by Liza and Grey. In a moment he wishes he could erase from his memory, Michael York was asked by Frost if he regretted that his character did not have any songs. In his autobiography, *Accidentally on Purpose*, York recalled how the curtain behind him suddenly rose to reveal a full orchestra and Frost turned to him and said, "Well, here's your chance to make up for that now!" York protested, but Frost insisted and eventually agreed to the actor's request to sing along with him.

Cabaret's Los Angeles premiere, held on April 5, 1972, was tied to the opening of a new cinema in the ABC Entertainment Center in Century City. Among the celebrity guests were Liza's father, Vincente Minnelli, and Desi Jr.'s mother, Lucille Ball, who were greeted by a mob of fans.

"A-drama-with-music"

If the filmmakers, Allied Artists, and ABC Pictures were still not convinced that they had a surefire hit on their hands, then the first official review of *Cabaret*, published in *Variety* on February 11, 1972, must have left everyone, even a self-admitted pessimist and cynic like Fosse, feeling hopeful, if not optimistic: "The film version of 'Cabaret' is most unusual: it is literate, bawdy, sophisticated, sensual, cynical, heart-warming, and disturbingly sophisticated. Liza Minnelli heads a stronger cast that under Bob Fosse's generally excellent direction re-creates the milieu of Germany some 40 years ago."

The majority of the reviews that followed praised the film, Fosse, and his talented cast. They also distinguished *Cabaret* from other movie musicals, declaring that it would "serve as a yardstick for future musicals" (Charles Champlin, *Los Angeles Times*) and was certain to "make movie history" (Pauline Kael, the *New Yorker*). Some critics felt it was also necessary to explain *Cabaret's* place within the musical genre, thereby demonstrating just how narrow the parameters were back then as to what constitutes a film musical. *Variety* emphasized that *Cabaret* is not a traditional "film-musical" but "a-drama-with-music, a point which promotional campaigns must deal with adroitly." Roger Greenspan of the *New York Times* defined *Cabaret* as "not so much a movie musical as it is a movie with a lot of music in it." *The Hollywood Reporter*'s Gary Giddins hesitated to call it a musical, "since all of the music emanates logically from the Cabaret stage" and "characters who are not singers do not sing." Hollis Alpert, writing for the *Saturday Review*, also appreciated that "the only ones allowed to sing are those who *can* sing—clearly an innovation in musicals." Alpert was also one of many critics who preferred the film over the stage show, claiming, "they not only improved on the original, they have brilliantly transformed it." *The New Republic*'s Stanley Kauffman agreed: "The Isherwood original is incomparably the best; but the film musical is much better than the stage musical, is much better cast than it was on Broadway, and uses the political atmosphere much more than a first-act curtain."

On the whole, the reviews considered the cast to be uniformly first-rate, particularly Joel Grey in his tour-de-force portrayal of the Emcee. Liza was of course a revelation because most film critics had never heard her sing. Critics were blown away not only by her singing voice, particularly her rendition of the title song, but also by her acting talent. *Boxoffice*, a trade publication, which, as its title suggests, sees everything in terms of dollar signs, said, "her performance makes her the leading contender as the Super Star of the Seventies." Any negative criticism had more to do with the fact that Liza was too talented to be playing the role of a second-rate cabaret singer. Christopher Isherwood raised this point when asked his opinion of the film: "You have this little girl saying, 'Oh, I'll never make it. I haven't really any talent.' Then she comes to the stage and you realize that she's every inch Judy Garland's daughter. And Joel Grey comes on stage and he's simply fantastic. The truth is that this cabaret would have attracted half of Europe. You wouldn't have been able to get in for months on end."

The film's PG rating did not go unnoticed. Vernon Scott, a reporter for United Press International, used *Cabaret* as an example to demonstrate how the Hollywood film industry was inviting "government censorship or some other meddlesome control of its product by mislabeling movies." Scott claimed that *Cabaret*'s PG rating is misleading because it is a musical, so one expects "chunky home goodness, Julie Andrews, and Barbra Streisand," not "illegal abortions, homosexuality, [and] nudity." (For the record, there is only one illegal abortion; Max and Brian are technically bisexuals, not homosexuals; and there is no nudity, partial or otherwise, in *Cabaret*.) Richard Schickel of *Life*, one of the few who was critical of the musical's translation from stage to screen, felt the filmmakers did not go far enough in capturing the grotesque decadence. Schickel accused Fosse of erring on the "side of timidity" and taking a "self-conserving and audience-protection approach." "They got their PG rating, all right," Schickel concluded, "but I'm afraid they lost me." In a piece for the *New York Times*, critic Stephen Farber agreed with Schickel that the film had to "settle for conventional resolutions. The film teases us, but it stops short of challenging us." At the same time, Farber believed that even with its "PG rating 'Cabaret' deserves to be called the first adult musical."

"Everybody loves a winner"

The critical acclaim *Cabaret* received translated into dollars and cents at the box office. In its first five weeks, *Cabaret* grossed over $2 million. By the end of January 1973, the domestic box-office total surpassed $25 million and the *Hollywood Reporter* predicted the figure would continue to climb. In that same month, *Cabaret* started the 1973 awards season off on a high note, receiving a total of nine Golden Globe nominations and winning three major awards: Best Motion Picture—Musical/Comedy, Best Motion Picture

Actress—Musical/Comedy (Liza Minnelli), and Best Supporting Actor—Motion Picture (Joel Grey). For Allied Artists President Manny Wolf, the Golden Globe wins were important because they established *Cabaret* as a "critics' picture." "It is something which has never really been done in filmmaking," he explained to the *Hollywood Reporter*. "'Cabaret' is essentially the first dramatic film musical, and that's the distinction which makes a very unique item of the picture."

Cabaret's status as a serious Oscar contender became official when nominations were announced in Los Angeles on February 12, 1973. The musical received 10 nominations, the same number as its chief competitor, *The Godfather*, Francis Ford Coppola's adaptation of Mario Puzo's best-seller about an Italian American crime family. *The Godfather* opened to phenomenal reviews and was breaking box-office records. It initially received 11 nominations, but composer Nino Rota's nomination for Best Music, Original Dramatic Score was withdrawn because portions of it had been used in the 1958 Italian film *Fortunella*. In addition, three cast members—James Caan, Robert Duvall, and Al Pacino—were competing for Best Actor in a Supporting Role, so technically the most statues *The Godfather* could take home was eight.

The Godfather was considered the front-runner, so producer Cy Feuer thought *Cabaret* could maybe win one or two awards. But he grew more hopeful as the night wore on. The film won in all the technical categories. Joel Grey won and then Minnelli. When Fosse beat Coppola for Best Director, Feuer thought maybe the film had a chance. After hearing Fosse's acceptance speech, Feuer also had a personal reason for wanting the opportunity to go up to the podium.

When accepting his Academy Award for Best Director, Fosse thanked the principal cast members, Martin Baum, Gwen Verdon, and others, and then added: "I would also like to mention the producer, Cy Feuer, with whom I had a lot of disputes, but on a night like this you start having affection for everybody. Thank you."

Cabaret then lost Best Picture to *The Godfather*, so Feuer never had a chance to publicly respond that evening and perhaps mend bridges. In his memoirs, he lamented, "It was the most disappointing moment of my professional life. I missed winning an Oscar, but more important, I lost a chance to win back my friend."

CHAPTER 6

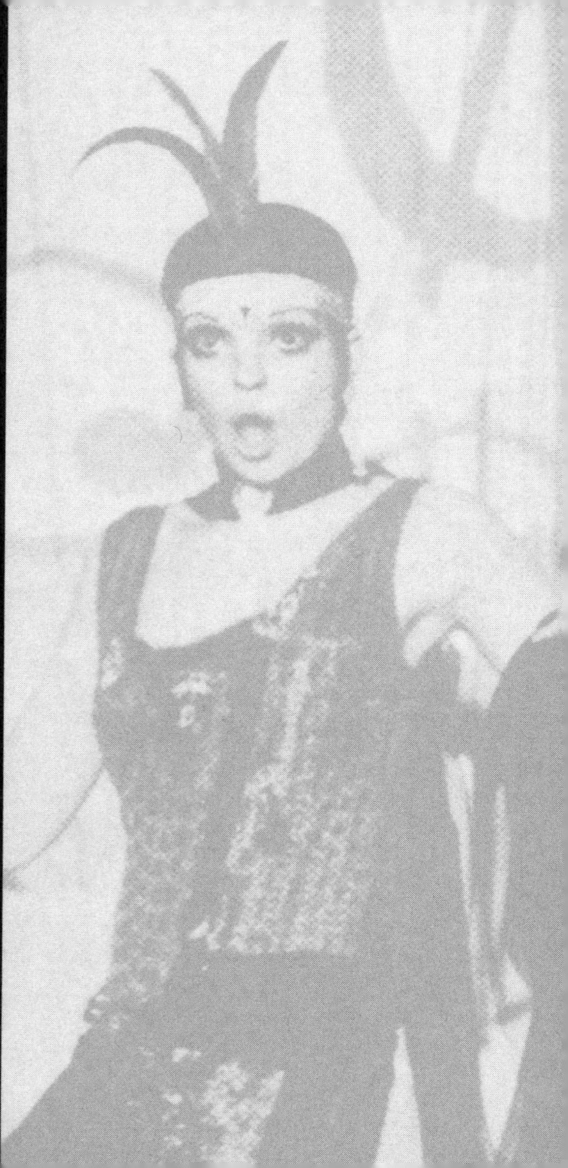

Cabaret
A Landmark Musical

The story of *Cabaret* does not end with Bob Fosse's acceptance speech. Like its Oscar night rival, *The Godfather*, *Cabaret* continues to be recognized as a landmark film in the annals of American cinema. In 1995, the musical was added to the National Film Registry, a list of "culturally, historically, or aesthetically significant" American films selected by the U.S. National Film Preservation Board for preservation in the Library of Congress. In 2004, the American Film Institute (AFI) ranked the song "Cabaret" number 18 in its list of the top 100 songs in American cinema. Two years later, the film was ranked number 5 in the AFI's list of Top 100 Musicals. In 2007 the film was added to the AFI's list (at number 63) of the 100 Greatest American Movies Ever Made.

While *Cabaret* was playing in theaters, Liza, Fosse, Kander, and Ebb collaborated on another project, *Liza with a Z: A Concert for Television* (1972). The hour-long special, which was shot at the Lyceum Theatre in New York City on May 31, 1972, and aired September 10 on NBC, featured a mixture of old songs ("God Bless the Child," "Son of a Preacher Man," "Bye Bye Blackbird") and new material. Kander and Ebb wrote the title song, in which Liza gives the audience a lesson on how to pronounce her first and last names. Ebb also produced the show with Fosse, who directed and choreographed Liza and her energetic line of backup dancers. The evening closed with a medley from *Cabaret* consisting of the title song, "Willkommen," "Married," "Money, Money," and "Maybe This Time." Fosse, always the maverick, even when directing for television, chose to film (as opposed to videotape) the evening using eight cameras. *Liza with a Z* received excellent reviews and won a Peabody Award and four Emmys. Fosse won in three categories (for choreography, direction, and coproducing with Ebb), topping off a very lucrative award season for the director, who joined an elite group (to which Liza already belonged) of artists who had won the triple crown—the Tony, Oscar, and Emmy. When Liza added a special Grammy to her mantle in 1990, she became a member of an even more exclusive club (with only twelve members to date) who have won all four major awards.

Two years later, Fosse, Kander, and Ebb were the creative team behind Liza's three-week, sold-out engagement at the Winter Garden Theatre in New York, for which she won a special Tony Award "for adding lustre to the Broadway season." Liza briefly shared a marquee with the trio once again in August 1975 when she temporarily took over the role of Velma Kelly for Gwen Verdon in the original production of the musical *Chicago* (1975–77). Her association with Kander and Ebb would continue through two more stage musicals, *The Act* (1977–78) and *The Rink* (1984), and Fred Ebb directed and wrote the book for Liza's tribute to her father, *Minnelli on Minnelli* (1999–2000). Ebb and Kander also contributed songs to Liza's post-*Cabaret* films, including *Lucky Lady* (1975), *A Matter of Time* (1976), *New York, New York* (1977) (the title tune became her second "signature song"), and *Stepping Out* (1991).

Minnelli and Grey's musical partnership, which had begun on a soundstage in Germany in 1971, did not end at the Kit Kat Klub. The pair continued to share the stage, from an engagement at the Riviera Hotel in Las Vegas in 1972 while *Cabaret* was still playing in theaters to a national tour in 1981. More recently, Liza joined Grey onstage after a performance of *Wicked* (in which he originated the role of the Wizard) in

2004 to help raise money for Broadway Cares/Equity Fights AIDS and in 2007 for a benefit for the Kravis Center for the Performing Arts in West Palm Beach.

Grey's connection to *Cabaret* also included the first Broadway revival in 1987, directed by Hal Prince. With his name over the title and his face prominently displayed on the poster, Grey was promoted from supporting to leading player. He was also given an additional song, "I Don't Care Much," which had been cut from the original score (Herr Schultz's "*Meeskite*" was cut from this version, but Cliff picked up a new song, "Don't Go"). As in the film, Cliff (Gregg Edelman) is bisexual, though it is not as dramatic and integral to the plot as in the film—perhaps a sign of how the times have changed. The same can be said for the final line of "If You Could See Her" ("She wouldn't look Jewish at all"). Dan Sullivan, critic for the *Los Angeles Times*, reported that the line got a big laugh the night he reviewed the revival in Los Angeles, part of the show's national tour before heading to New York. A glowing review from the Associated Press said that the revival "confirms the show's landmark status. It remains one of a handful of musicals—'Gypsy' and 'A Chorus Line' come immediately to mind—that are as remarkable today as they were when they arrived in New York." *New York Times* critic Frank Rich was less impressed. He praised Grey's performance, yet sympathized with the unfair demands being made on the actor to carry the whole show for an otherwise underwhelming production and cast, which included Alyson Reed as Sally, Regina Resnik as Fraulein Schneider, and *Hogan's Heroes* star Werner Klemperer as Herr Schultz.

A second, more successful revival of *Cabaret* began in London at the Donmar Warehouse in 1993. Director Sam Mendes transformed the theater into the Kit Kat Klub and cast the audience, seated at tables, as the club's patrons. As Rob Marshall, who codirected the Broadway production with Mendes, explained, "This *Cabaret* is real, rough, and raw. The Kit Kat Klub is second-rate—even third-rate. You'll see the runs in the stockings, the broken light-bulbs, the tackiness under the thin veneer of glitz." The Emcee, played by Tony winner Alan Cumming, was a flirtatious, pansexual figure, who, though less demonic than Grey's Emcee, was perhaps more threatening to modern audiences because he defied the categories that society continues to impose on gender and sexuality. In the process, he also took the show's "sleaze factor" up a few notches (or is that *down* a few notches?).

Like most recent stage productions of *Cabaret*, the 1998 revival added two songs from the film, "Mein Herr" and "Maybe This Time." Perhaps that is what makes *Cabaret* a true landmark musical—the fact that the stage versions now incorporate elements of the film, whether it be additional songs, Cliff's bisexuality, or Sally's signature bowler hat.

CABARET-OGRAPHY

I Am a Camera (November 28, 1951–July 12, 1952; 214 performances). Written and directed by John Van Druten. Based on *The Berlin Stories* by Christopher Isherwood. Producer: Gertrude Macy. Scenic Design/Lighting Design: Boris Aronson. Costumes: Ellen Goldsborough. Cast: Julie Harris (Sally Bowles), William Prince (Christopher Isherwood), Edward Andrews (Clive Mortimer), Martin Brooks (Fritz Wendel), Olga Fabian (Fraulein Schneider), Catherine Willard (Mrs. Watson-Courtneidge), Marian Winters (Natalia Landauer).

Awards/Nominations: *Tony Awards*—Best Actress in a Play (Julie Harris, winner), Best Featured Actress in a Play (Marian Winters, winner), Theatre World Award (Marian Winters, winner).

I Am a Camera (1955). Directed by Henry Cornelius. Written by John Collier. Based on the play by John Van Druten and Christopher Isherwood's *Berlin Stories*. Music: Malcolm Arnold. Cinematography: Guy Green. Editor: Clive Donner. Art Direction: William Kellner. Cast: Julie Harris (Sally Bowles), Laurence Harvey (Christopher Isherwood), Shelley Winters (Natalia Landauer), Ron Randell (Clive), Lea Seidl (Fraulein Schneider), Anton Diffring (Fritz Wendel). Produced by Romulus Films. Distributed by Distributors Corporation of America.

Awards/Nominations: *BAFTA* (British Academy of Film and Television Arts)—Best Foreign Actress (Julie Harris, nominee).

Cabaret (November 2, 1966 [previews]/November 20, 1966 [opening]–September 6, 1969; 21 previews/1,165 performances). Produced and directed by Harold Prince. Produced in association with Ruth Mitchell. Book by Joe Masteroff. Based on the play *I Am a Camera* by John Van Druten. Based on stories by Christopher Isherwood. Music by John Kander. Lyrics by Fred Ebb. Choreographed by Ronald Field. Musical Director: Harold Hastings. Music orchestrated by Don Walker. Scenic Design: Boris Aronson. Costume Design: Patricia Zipprodt. Lighting Design: Jean Rosenthal. Cast: Bert Convy (Clifford Bradshaw), Jack Gilford (Herr Schultz), Jill

Haworth (Sally Bowles), Lotte Lenya (Fraulein Schneider), Joel Grey (Master of Ceremonies), Peg Murray (Fraulein Kost), Edward Winter (Ernst Ludwig).

Awards/Nominations: *Tony Awards*—Best Musical (Joseph Masteroff, John Kander, Fred Ebb, Harold Prince, Ruth Mitchell, winners), Best Composer and Lyrics (John Kander and Fred Ebb, winners), Best Actor in a Musical (Jack Gilford, nominee), Best Actress in a Musical (Lotte Lenya, nominee), Best Featured Actor in a Musical (Joel Grey, winner), Best Featured Actor in a Musical (Edward Winter, nominee), Best Featured Actress in a Musical (Peg Murray, winner), Best Scenic Design (Boris Aronson, winner), Best Costume Design (Patricia Zipprodt, winner), Best Choreography (Ronald Field, winner), Best Direction of a Musical (Harold Prince, winner).

Cabaret (1972). Directed by Bob Fosse. Produced by Cy Feuer. Screenplay by Jay Allen. Based on the musical play *Cabaret* by Joe Masteroff, the play *I Am a Camera* by John Van Druten, and the stories of Christopher Isherwood. Original music by John Kander. Lyrics by Fred Ebb. Cinematography: Geoffrey Unsworth. Editing: David Bretherton. Production Design: Rolf Zehetbauer. Art Director: Jurgen Kiebach. Cast: Liza Minnelli (Sally Bowles), Michael York (Brian Roberts), Helmut Griem (Maximilian von Heune), Joel Grey (Master of Ceremonies), Fritz Wepper (Fritz Wendel), Marisa Berenson (Natalia Landauer), Kathryn Doby, Inge Jaeger, Angelika Koch, Helen Velkovorska, Gitta Schmidt, and Louise Quick (The Kit Kat Dancers).

THE SONGS

"Willkommen" . . . . Emcee, Kit Kat Girls, ensemble
"Mein Herr". . . . . Sally Bowles
"Maybe This Time". . . . . Sally Bowles
"Money, Money". . . . . .Emcee, Sally Bowles
"Two Ladies" . . . . Emcee and Dancers
"Sitting Pretty" . . . . .Kit Kat Klub orchestra
"Tomorrow Belongs to Me" . . . . . Nazis, *Biergarten* staff and patrons
"Tiller Girls" .Kit Kat Klub orchestra
"*Heiraten*" (Married) . . . . .Greta Keller
"If You Could See Her" . . . . Emcee
"Cabaret" . . . . Sally Bowles
"Finale". . . . . Emcee

Awards/Nominations: *Academy Awards*—Best Actor in a Supporting Role (Joel Grey, winner), Best Actress in a Leading Role (Liza Minnelli, winner), Best Art Direction/ Set Decoration (Rolf Zehetbauer, Hans Jürgen Kiebach, Herbert Strabel, winners), Best Cinematography (Geoffrey

Unsworth, winner), Best Director (Bob Fosse, winner), Best Film Editing (David Bretherton, winner), Best Music, Scoring Original Song Score and/or Adaptation (Ralph Burns, winner), Best Sound (Robert Knudson, David Hildyard, winners), Best Picture (Cy Feuer, nominee), Best Writing, Screenplay Based on Material from Another Medium (Jay Allen, nominee). *BAFTA*—Best Actress (Liza Minnelli, winner), Best Art Direction (Rolf Zehetbauer, winner), Best Cinematography (Geoffrey Unsworth, winner), Best Direction (Bob Fosse, winner), Best Film, Best Sound Track (David Hildyard, Robert Knudson, Arthur Piantadosi, winners), Most Promising Newcomer to Leading Film Roles (Joel Grey, winner), Best Costume Design (Charlotte Flemming, nominee), Best Film Editing (David Bretherton, nominee), Best Screenplay (Jay Allen, nominee), Best Supporting Actress (Marisa Berenson, nominee). *Golden Globes*—Best Motion Picture—Music/Comedy (winner), Best Motion Picture Actress—Music/Comedy (Liza Minnelli, winner), Best Supporting Actor—Motion Picture (Joel Grey, winner), Best Original Song, "Mein Herr" and "Money, Money" (John Kander and Fred Ebb, nominees), Best Screenplay (Jay Allen, nominee), Best Supporting Actress—Motion Picture (Marisa Berenson, nominee), Most Promising Newcomer—Female (Marisa Berenson, nominee). *National Board of Review*— Best Director (Bob Fosse, winner), Best Film (winner), Best

Supporting Actor (Joel Grey, winner, tied with Al Pacino, *The Godfather*), Best Supporting Actress (Marisa Berenson, winner). *National Society of Film Critics*—Best Supporting Actor (Joel Grey, winner, tied with Eddie Albert, *The Heartbreak Kid*).

Cabaret (October 7, 1987 [previews]/October 22, 1987 [opening]–June 4, 1988; 18 previews/261 performances). Directed by Harold Prince. Dance and Cabaret Numbers Staged by Ron Field. Book by Joe Masteroff. Based on the play by John Van Druten. Based on stories by Christopher Isherwood. Music by John Kander. Lyrics by Fred Ebb. Produced by Barry and Fran Weissler. Produced in association with Phil Witt. Scenic Design: David Chapman. Costume Design: Patricia Zipprodt. Lighting Design: Marc B. Weiss. Based on original set designs by Boris Aronson. Cast: Joel Grey (Master of Ceremonies), Gregg Edelman (Clifford Bradshaw), Werner Klemperer (Herr Schultz), Nora Mae Lyng (Fraulein Kost), Alyson Reed (Sally Bowles), Regina Resnik (Fraulein Schneider), David Staller (Ernst Ludwig).

Awards/Nominations: *Tony Awards*—Best Featured Actor (Werner Klemperer, nominee), Best Featured Actress in a Musical (Alyson Reed, nominee), Best Featured Actress in a Musical (Regina Resnick, nominee), Best Revival (Barry and Fran Weissler, nominees). *Drama Desk*

Awards—Outstanding Actor in a Musical (Joel Grey, nominee), Outstanding Director of a Musical (Harold Prince, nominee). Outstanding Revival (Barry and Fran Weissler, Phil Witt, nominees).

Cabaret (February 13, 1998 [previews]/March 19, 1998 [opening]–January 4, 2004; 37 previews/2,377 performances). Directed by Sam Mendes. Codirected and choreographed by Rob Marshall. Inspired by the 1993 production of *Cabaret* at The Donmar Warehouse, directed by Sam Mendes. Produced by The Roundabout Theatre Company. Book by Joe Masteroff. Music by John Kander. Lyrics by Fred Ebb. Based on the play by John Van Druten. Based on stories by Christopher Isherwood. Musical Director: Patrick Vaccariello. Set and Club Design: Robert Brill. Costume Design: William Ivey Long. Lighting Design: Peggy Eisenhauer and Mike Baldassari. Sound Design: Brian Ronan. Make-up and Hair Design: Randy Mercer. Cast: Alan Cumming (Master of Ceremonies), Natasha Richardson (Sally Bowles), Ron Rifkin (Herr Schultz), John Benjamin Hickey (Clifford Bradshaw), Denis O'Hare (Ernst Ludwig), Michele Pawk (Fraulein Kost/Fritzie), Mary Louise Wilson (Fraulein Schneider).

Awards/Nominations: *Tony Awards*—Best Revival (winner), Best Actor in a Musical (Alan Cumming, winner), Best Actress in a Musical (Natasha Richardson, winner),

Best Featured Actor in a Musical (Ron Rifkin, winner), Best Featured Actress in a Musical (Mary Louise Wilson, nominee), Best Costume Design (William Ivey Long, nominee), Best Lighting Design (Peggy Eisenhauer, Mike Baldasarri, nominees), Best Choreography (Rob Marshall, nominee), Best Director of a Musical (Sam Mendes and Rob Marshall, nominees). *Drama Desk Awards*—Outstanding Revival of a Musical (winner), Outstanding Actor in a Musical (Alan Cumming, winner), Outstanding Actress in a Musical (Natasha Richardson, winner), Outstanding Featured Actress in a Musical (Michele Pawk, nominee), Outstanding Choreography (Rob Marshall, nominee), Outstanding Direction of a Musical (Sam Mendes and Rob Marshall, nominees), Outstanding Orchestrations (Michael Gibson, nominee), Outstanding Set Design of a Musical (Robert Brill, nominee), Outstanding Costume Design (William Ivey Long, nominee), Outstanding Lighting Design (Peggy Eisenhauer, Mike Baldassari, nominees). *Theatre World Award*—Alan Cumming (winner).

NOTES

1. "Willkommen, Bienvenue, Welcome"

3 According to critic: Gary Giddins, "'Cabaret' on Film," *The Hollywood Reporter*, February 15, 1972, 3.

5 To cover the: "ABC Picts. Splits 'Cabaret' Neg Tab with AA, 'Mame' with WB," *Variety*, January 22, 1970, 1.

7 Two weeks: "Liza—Fire, Air and a Touch of Anguish," *Time*, February 28, 1972, 65–71; "Liza Minnelli: A Star is Born," *Newsweek*, February 28, 1972, 82–86.

2. Chris and Sally

12 As Isherwood once: Winston Leyland, "Christopher Isherwood Interview," in *Conversations with Christopher Isherwood*, ed. James J. Berg and Chris Freeman (Jackson: University of Mississippi Press, 2001), 98.

13   According to Isherwood: David J. Gehrin, "An Interview with Christopher Isherwood," in Berg and Freeman, *Conversations with Christopher Isherwood*, 75.

14   "The sun shines": Christopher Isherwood, *Goodbye to Berlin*, in Isherwood, *The Berlin Stories* (reprint) (New York: New Directions, 2008), 207.

15   Historian Peter Jelavich: Peter Jelavich, *Berlin Cabaret* (Cambridge, MA: Harvard University Press, 1993), 2.

15   He describes the "ideal cabaret": Jelavich, *Berlin Cabaret*, 2.

16   The character of: Isherwood, *Goodbye to Berlin*, 25.

16   Christopher describes it: Isherwood, *Goodbye to Berlin*, 192.

16   Outside they: Isherwood, *Goodbye to Berlin*, 193.

17   "Berlin meant boys": Christopher Isherwood, *Christopher and His Kind 1929–1939* (New York: Avon, 1976), 2, 3.

17   Isherwood claimed: Isherwood, *Christopher and His Kind*, 3.

17   There is no mention: Isherwood, *Christopher and His Kind*, 40–45.

19   "She was dressed": Isherwood, *Goodbye to Berlin*, 22.

19   The next time: Isherwood, *Goodbye to Berlin*, 25.

NOTES 115

21 According to Isherwood's: Peter Parker, *Isherwood: A Life Revealed* (New York: Random House, 2004), 179–180.

21 Unlike Sally's: Isherwood, *Christopher and His Kind*, 62.

22 Isherwood characterized: Leyland, "Christopher Isherwood Interview," 103.

22 Years later: Christopher Isherwood, "The Faces of Sally Bowles," *The Times*, August 16, 1975, 5.

22 Before publishing: Isherwood, "The Faces of Sally Bowles," 5.

23 In addition to working: Linda Mizejewski, *Divine Decadence: Fascism, Female Spectacle, and the Makings of Sally Bowles* (Princeton, NJ: Princeton University Press, 1992), 44–45.

23 Minnelli thinks: Liza Minnelli, interview with author, August 25, 2010.

23 According to Ross': Sarah Caudwell, "Reply to Berlin," *New Statesman*, October 3, 1986, 28.

23 When a revival: Caudwell, "Reply to Berlin," 28.

23 Caudwell explained: Caudwell, "Reply to Berlin," 28.

24 "I wish I could": Isherwood, *Christopher and His Kind*, 59.

25 Isherwood claimed that: Isherwood, *Christopher and His Kind*, 58.

25 When Christopher departs: Isherwood, *Goodbye to Berlin*, 206.

25 Although Isherwood had: Isherwood, *Goodbye to Berlin*, 206–207.

25 Nineteen years: Isherwood, *Christopher and His Kind*, 131.

27 According to Isherwood's: Parker, *Isherwood: A Life Revealed*, 179.

28 Natalia's father: Studs Terkel, "Christopher Isherwood," in Berg and Freeman, *Conversations with Christopher Isherwood*, 173–174.

29 "I am a camera": Isherwood, *Goodbye to Berlin*, 1.

29 Isherwood claims: Isherwood, *Christopher and His Kind*, 57.

29 Unfortunately, the metaphor: Isherwood, *Christopher and His Kind*, 57.

30 His decision to: George Wickes, "An Interview with Christopher Isherwood," in Berg and Freeman, *Conversations with Christopher Isherwood*, 27.

30 Isherwood's favorite moment: Gehrin, "An Interview with Christopher Isherwood," 78.

31 Citing Chekhov and: John Van Druten, "Mood of the Moment," *New York Times*, November 25, 1951, 121.

31 In his introduction: John Van Druten, "Note to Producers," *I Am a Camera* (New York: Dramatists Play Service, 1983), 5–6.

32   "A play that has no center": "The Theatre: New Play in
       Manhattan, December 10, 1951," *Time*, December 10,
       1951.

32   "A little obvious and immature": Wolcott Gibbons, "The
       Nether Regions," *The New Yorker*, December 8, 1951, 62.

32   "Never . . . dull": Brooks Atkinson, "At The Theatre,"
       New York Times, November 29, 1951, 38.

32   "Me no Leica": Walter Kerr, *New York Herald*, Decem-
       ber 31, 1951.

32   "Brilliant performance": Gibbons, "The Nether Re-
       gions," 62.

32   "With amazing verve": "The Theatre: New Play in Man-
       hattan, Dec. 10, 1951."

32   "A virtuosity and": Atkinson, "At The Theatre," 38.

32   Attributing the: Isherwood, *Christopher and His Kind*,
       60.

33   In other words: Iain Johnstone, "The Real Sally Bowles,"
       Folio, Autumn 1975, 35.

33   Harris also saw: Johnstone, "The Real Sally Bowles," 35.

34   *I Am a Camera* was denied: Geoffrey M. Shurlock,
       letter to Irving Wormser, July 21, 1955, *I Am a Camera*
       Production Code Administration File, Department of
       Special Collections, Margaret Herrick Library, Acad-
       emy of Motion Pictures Arts and Sciences, Beverly
       Hills, California.

34 *I Am a Camera* still failed: Geoffrey M. Shurlock, letter to Fred J. Schwartz, December 31, 1956, *I Am a Camera* Production Code Administration File.

34 The film was also: "Legion of Decency Nix on 'Camera' is Appealed to Cardinal Spellman," *The Hollywood Reporter*, August 15, 1955.

35 Once again: Bosley Crowther, "Screen: 'I Am a Camera,'" *New York Times*, August 9, 1955, 29.

3. "Divine Decadence"

37 Once Prince: Carol Ilson, *Harold Prince: A Director's Journey* (New York: Limelight, 2000), 138.

38 Kander and Ebb wrote: Hal Prince, *Contradictions: Notes on Twenty-six Years in the* Theatre (New York: Dodd, Mead, 1974), 126.

38 Minnelli recalls that: Liza Minnelli, interview with author, August 25, 2010.

38 In his autobiography: Prince, *Contradictions*, 125–126.

40 Prince considers the: Prince, *Contradictions*, 127–130.

41 I suggested splitting: Prince, *Contradictions*, 130–131.

41 Scenic designer: Prince, *Contradictions*, 133.

42 Fred Ebb, who said: "Cabaret," *Broadway Song and Story*, ed. Otis L. Guernsey Jr. (New York: Dodd, Mead, 1985), 141.

43 The original line: "Cabaret," *Broadway Song and Story*, 142.

43 Kander listened: Greg Lawrence, *Colored Lights: Forty Years of Words and Music, Show Biz, Collaboration, and All That Jazz* (New York: Faber and Faber, 2003), 63.

43 When Kander explained: Lawrence, *Colored Lights*, 68–69.

44 The participation of: Rex Reed, "The Lady Known as Lenya," *New York Times*, November 20, 1966, 136.

44 Joel Grey, who: Joel Grey, interview with author, August 23, 2010.

44 Considering her roots: Reed, "The Lady Known as Lenya," 142.

44 According to one: Leonard Lyons, "Julie Andrews Turns Down Star Role in Movie 'Camelot,'" *Salt Lake Tribune*, April 6, 1966, B3: Leonard Lyons, "Edward G. Robinson Imitates Self," *Salt Lake Tribune*, June 14, 1966.

45 Grey thinks: Grey, interview with author, August 23, 2010.

45 Masteroff recalls: "Cabaret," *Broadway Song and Story*, 145.

45 Haworth, who was: Johnstone, "The Real Sally Bowles," 35.

45 Judi Dench, who played: Johnstone, "The Real Sally Bowles," 35–36.

46 The most influential: Walter Kerr, "The Theatre: 'Cabaret' Opens at the Broadhurst," *New York Times*, November 21, 1966, 62.

47 In the summer: "Cinerama Buys 'Cabaret' for $2 Mil-Plus," *Variety*, July 31, 1968.

47 Seven months later: "Cinerama, Prince Deal for Filming 'Cabaret' Off," *The Hollywood Reporter*, February 27, 1969.

47 The rights to *Cabaret*: "AA Pays $1.5 Mil for 'Cabaret,'" *Variety*, May 28, 1969, 1.

47 In January 1970: "ABC Picts. Splits 'Cabaret' Neg Tab with AA, 'Mame' with WB," *Variety*, January 22, 1970, 1.

48 ABC Pictures President: "ABC Picts. Splits 'Cabaret,'" 22.

48 Hoping to expand: Cy Feuer with Ken Gross, *I Got the Show Right Here* (New York: Applause, 2005), 239.

49 As Feuer later explained: Feuer, *I Got the Show Right Here*, 240.

50 "There can be no": Feuer, *I Got the Show Right Here*, 241.

51 As Fosse explained in: Paul Gardner, "Bob Fosse on His Toes," *New York*, December 16, 1974, 59.

51 "As I saw it": Feuer, *I Got the Show Right Here*, 243.

52 *Variety* called it: "'Sweet Charity'" (review), *Variety*, December 31, 1931.

53 Many of them: Vincent Canby, "Screen: A Blow-up of 'Sweet Charity,'" *New York Times*, April 2, 1969, 38.

53 In an article: Vincent Canby, "Is the Cost of 'Charity' Too High?" *New York Times*, April 6, 1969, D1.

56 "I can certainly understand": Judith Crist, *Take 22: Moviemakers on Moviemaking* (New York: Continuum, 1991), 304.

56 In the end, all: Cy Feuer, letter to Wilfred E. Dodd, October 6, 1970, Bob Fosse and Gwen Verdon Collection, Special Collections, Music Division, Library of Congress, Box 16B.

57 Feuer's memo summarizing: Feuer, letter to Wilfred E. Dodd, October 6, 1970, Bob Fosse and Gwen Verdon Collection.

58 Meanwhile, Fosse had given: Script Notes, Bob Fosse and Gwen Verdon Collection, Box 16B, Folder 11.

59 As Jay Allen: Crist, *Take 22*, 303.

60 In an interview given: Joyce Gabriel, "Liza Finally Sings Role She Wanted," *The Cumberland Times*, February 27, 1972, 22.

61 Liza recalled that they: Gabriel, "Liza Finally Sings Role She Wanted," 22.

61 In an interview for *Penthouse*: Lionel Chetwynd, "Except for Bob Fosse," *Penthouse*, January 1974, 92.

61 Baum and Feuer made: Grey, interview with author, August 23, 2010.

62 Michael York had heard: "*Cabaret*: A Legend in the Making," *Cabaret* (Special Edition), dir. Bob Fosse, perf. Liza Minnelli, Joel Grey, Michael York, Warner Brothers, 1998.

62 Other actors considered: Casting notes, Bob Fosse and Gwen Verdon Collection, Box 16C, Folder 4.

62 Fosse later admitted: Chetwynd, "Except for Bob Fosse," 92.

62 In mid-November: Casting notes, Bob Fosse and Gwen Verdon Collection, Box 16C, Folder 4.

62 "I've never seen anyone": Chetwynd, "Except for Bob Fosse," 92.

63 "We are all bisexual": Edward Portnoy, "Helmut Griem and 'Children of Rage,'" *After Dark*, December 1974, 46.

64 Minnelli recalls: Minnelli, interview with author, August 25, 2010.

64 When they finished shooting: Rex Reed, "Liza Minnelli: Her 'Cabaret' Will Be Like it WAS," *San Antonio Light*, July 25, 1971, 23.

64 Whether Feuer did or did not: Feuer, *I Got the Show Right Here*, 246–248.

65　In a 1974 interview: Chetwynd, "Except for Bob Fosse," 92.

65　"We were told": John Kander, interview with author, September 22, 2010.

4. Shooting *Cabaret*

68　In the production notes: *Cabaret* production notes, *Cabaret* press file, Margaret Herrick Library, Academy of Motion Picture Arts and Sciences, Beverly Hills, California.

68　In an interview with: Lil Picard, "Inter/view with Bob Fosse," *Interview*, March 1972.

69　"He had a vision": Liza Minnelli, interview with author, August 25, 2010.

69　Dancer Louise Quick: Louise Quick, interview with author, August 27, 2010.

70　"Fosse read the note": Minnelli, interview with author, August 25, 2010.

71　In an effort: Glenn Loney, "The Many Facets of Bob Fosse," *After Dark*, June 1972, 46.

71　For Minnelli: Minnelli, interview with author, August 25, 2010.

71　Minnelli did consult: Rex Reed, "Liza Minnelli: Her 'Cabaret' Will Be Like it WAS," *San Antonio Light*, July 25, 1971, 23.

72 "The first ones [costumes]": Robert Colaciello and Glenn O'Brien, "Inter/view with Marisa Berenson," *Interview*, March 1972, 6.

72 "My German": Joel Grey, interview with author, August 23, 2010.

72 When Liza asked: Reed, "Liza Minnelli: Her 'Cabaret' Will Be Like it WAS," 23.

73 "They mistrusted how": Grey, interview with author, August 23, 2010.

73 Liza recalls that: Minnelli, interview with author, August 25, 2010.

75 "Some of the Germans": Vic Heutschy, interview with author, August 20, 2010.

75 "Eventually, as I": Picard, "Inter/view with Bob Fosse."

75 "In the final shooting," Jay Presson Allen and Hugh Wheeler, *Cabaret* (Final Draft), February 15, 1971, Bob Fosse and Gwen Verdon Collection, Special Collections, Music Division, Library of Congress, Box 15C, Folder 1.

76 "While the technicians": Michael York, *Accidentally on Purpose* (New York: Simon & Schuster, 1991), 274.

76 York found Fosse: Gordon Gow, "Something Dynamic," *Films & Filming*, May 1974, 21.

77 Marisa Berenson was: Colaciello and O'Brien, "Inter/view with Marisa Berenson," 6.

77 To get her: As qtd. in "*Cabaret*: A Legend in the Making," *Cabaret* (Special Edition), dir. Bob Fosse, perf. Liza Minnelli, Joel Grey, Michael York, Warner Brothers, 1998.

77 "They were scared": Quick, interview with author, August 27, 2010.

78 Publicist Vic: Heutschy, interview with author, August 20, 2010.

78 Heutschy said: Heutschy, interview with author, August 20, 2010.

78 One welcomed visitor: Heutschy, interview with author, August 20, 2010.

80 As Bretherton told it: "David Bretherton," *Selected Takes: Film Editors on Editing*, ed. Vincent Lobrutto (Westport, CT: Praeger, 1991), 56.

81 "All of a sudden": "David Bretherton," 56.

83 "I have just seen": Martin Gottfried, *All His Jazz: The Life and Death of Bob Fosse* (New York: DaCapo Press, 1990), 227–228.

5. "Life *Is* a Cabaret"

86 Approximately 70 percent: Lewis J. Rachmil, Memo to Distribution, American Broadcasting Company, February 4, 1972, Bob Fosse and Gwen Verdon Col-

lection, Special Collections, Music Division, Library of Congress, Box 16B, Folder 16.

86   Most people summed up: Preview Cards, Bob Fosse and Gwen Verdon Collection, Box 16B, Folder 16.

89   In the version: Jay Presson Allen and Hugh Wheeler, *Cabaret* (Final Draft), February 15, 1971, Bob Fosse and Gwen Verdon Collection, Special Collections, Music Division, Library of Congress, Box 15C, Folder 1.

89   "Outraged by the request": Michael York, *Accidentally on Purpose* (New York: Simon & Schuster, 1991), 276.

90   In a moment: York, *Accidentally on Purpose*, 290–291.

91   *Cabaret*'s Los Angeles: Jody Jacobs, "Stars Come to the 'Cabaret' for Premiere," *Los Angeles Times*, April 7, 1972.

91   "The film version of 'Cabaret'": Murph, "'Cabaret'" (review) *Daily Variety*, February 11, 1972.

91   "Serve as a yardstick": Charles Champlin, "'Cabaret' a Yardstick for Future Musicals," *Los Angeles Times*, April 2, 1972, O1.

91   "Make movie history": Pauline Kael, "Grinning," *The New Yorker*, February 19, 1972, 84.

92   "*Variety* emphasized" Murph, "'Cabaret.'"

92   Roger Greenspan of: Roger Greenspan, "Liza Minnelli Stirs a Lively 'Cabaret,'" *New York Times*, February 14, 1972, 22.

92 *The Hollywood Reporter*'s: Giddins, "'Cabaret' on Film," 3, 9.

92 Hollis Alpert, writing for: Hollis Alpert, "Willkommen, Bienvenue, Welcome," *Saturday Review*, March 4, 1972.

92 Alpert was also one: Alpert, "Willkommen, Bienvenue, Welcome."

92 *The New Republic*'s: Stanley Kauffman, "'Cabaret'" (review), *The New Republic*, March 4, 1972, 22.

93 *Boxoffice*: "Cabaret," *Boxoffice*, February 28, 1972.

93 "You have this little girl": Gehrin, "An Interview with Christopher Isherwood," 78.

93 Vernon Scott, a reporter: Vernon Scott, "Movie Ratings Called Boondoggle," *Press-Telegram* (Long Beach, CA), April 10, 1972, 12.

93 Scott claimed: Scott, "Movie Ratings Called Boondoggle," 12.

94 Schickel accused Fosse: Richard Schickel, "Liza Minnelli Sallies Fourth," *Life*, March 10, 1972, 24.

94 In a piece for: Stephen Farber, 'Cabaret' May Shock Kansas," *New York Times*, February 20, 1972, D1.

94 By the end of January: "'Cabaret' Grosses 25.8 Mil to Date in Domestic Houses," *The Hollywood Reporter*, January 26, 1973.

95 For Allied Artists President: Will Tusher, "'Cabaret' B.O. Jingles $40 Mil Money Song," *The Hollywood Reporter*, January 31, 1973.

96 In his memoirs: Feuer, *I Got the Show Right Here*, 253.

6. *Cabaret*

102 Dan Sullivan, critic: Dan Sullivan, "Welcome to 'Cabaret'—for a New Generation," *Los Angeles Times*, June 22, 1987, C3.

102 A glowing review: Michael Kuchwara, "A Revival of 'Cabaret' Starring Joel Grey Opens on Broadway," *The News* (Frederick, MD), October 23, 1987, D-1.

102 *New York Times* critic: Frank Rich, "Theatre: 'Cabaret' and Joel Grey Return," *New York Times*, October 23, 1987, C3.

103 As Rob Marshall: *Cabaret: The Illustrated Book and Lyrics* (New York: Newmarket Press, 1999), 20.

INDEX